ON THE MEDIEVAL ORIGINS OF
THE MODERN STATE

ON THE
Medieval Origins of
THE MODERN STATE

JOSEPH R. STRAYER

PRINCETON UNIVERSITY PRESS
PRINCETON, NEW JERSEY

Copyright © 1970 by Princeton University Press
ALL RIGHTS RESERVED
Library of Congress Card: 79-113011
International Standard Book Number: 0-691-05183-6

First Princeton Paperback Printing, 1973

Publication of this book has been aided
by a grant from the Whitney Darrow
Publication Reserve Fund
of Princeton University Press

This book has been composed in Linotype Caledonia
Printed in the United States of America
by Princeton University Press

Preface

THIS BOOK is based on the Witherspoon Lectures given at Princeton University in 1961 at the invitation of the Undergraduate Council. Some of the ideas were further developed in a paper on medieval bureaucracy and the modern state, read at the 1965 meeting of the American Political Science Association. Since I had had to cover the later Middle Ages very hastily in the Witherspoon Lectures, I welcomed an opportunity to discuss this period more thoroughly in an essay read at the 1968 Conference of the Center for Medieval and Early Renaissance Studies of the State University of New York at Binghamton. This essay will be included in the forthcoming publication of the proceedings of the Conference. I am grateful to the University, and to Professor Bernard S. Levy, Conference Coordinator, for permission to use some of the material presented at Binghamton in this book.

These formal acknowledgments do not begin to express the debt that I owe to my students and to my colleagues. A book that grows out of teaching, as this one did, has been shaped by the comments, the inquiries, and the criticisms of hundreds of people. The give and take of academic debate has stimulated my thinking and has forced me to clarify my ideas. It has encouraged me to look for broad patterns in the intricate and often confusing details of institutional history. Finally, it was the teaching experience that convinced me that I could say something useful about a vast subject in a small number of pages.

If the book grew out of my teaching, the teaching in

turn grew out of my research. This is why the book emphasizes topics that I have studied in some detail and skips rapidly over other matters that may be equally important. The most obvious example of such a bias is my concentration on the institutions of France and England. There is some reason for this emphasis, as I try to show in the text. The first European states that have endured to our own time were formed in France and England, and all other European states were strongly influenced by the example of these precursors. In any case France and England offer excellent, if not unique, examples of the process of state-building.

The purpose of the book is to explain how European states developed some of the institutions that have made them such powerful instruments for organizing and controlling large bodies of men. The reader should remember that to describe a phenomenon is not to praise it. I do not believe that the chief end of man is to create states or that all means of preserving and strengthening states are desirable. I do believe that the state has succeeded in getting large numbers of men to work together effectively, and that the state can embody human ideals and human aspirations just as well as any other form of social organization. Co-operation in the effort to achieve common goals has been responsible for most human achievements, and the state offers one way of securing this cooperation. It is certainly not the only way of securing cooperation, but at present it is the dominant way. There is some reason, then, to try to see what the state is and how it became what it is.

Princeton, New Jersey   JOSEPH R. STRAYER
November 1969

ON THE MEDIEVAL ORIGINS OF
THE MODERN STATE

i

𝕵𝖔𝖉𝖆𝖞 we take the state for granted. We grumble about its demands; we complain that it is encroaching more and more on what used to be our private concerns, but we can hardly envisage life without it. In the world of today, the worst fate that can befall a human being is to be stateless. Hale's "man without a country" does exist now, and he is wretched in ways which Hale could never imagine. The old forms of social identification are no longer absolutely necessary. A man can lead a reasonably full life without a family, a fixed local residence, or a religious affiliation, but if he is stateless he is nothing. He has no rights, no security, and little opportunity for a useful career. There is no salvation on earth outside the framework of an organized state.

This was not always so. There were periods—not long ago as historians measure time—when the state did not exist, and when no one was concerned that it did not exist. In those times it was the man without a family or a lord, without membership in a local community or a dominant religious group, who had no security and no opportunity, who could survive only by becoming a servant or a slave. The values of this kind of a society were different from ours; the supreme sacrifices of property and life were made for family, lord, community, or religion, not for the state. The organizing power of such societies was less than ours; it was difficult to get very many people to work together for any length of time. There was a strong sense of reciprocal obligation among those who knew each other personally, but this sense of obligation faded rapidly with distance. Imperfect and spatially limited types of organization meant that the society could not make the best use of its human and natural resources, that its level of living was low, and that capable individuals were unable to realize their full potentialities. The development of the modern state, on the other hand, made possible such a concentrated use of human resources that no other type of social organization could avoid being relegated to a subordinate role. We pay a price—sometimes a dangerously high price—for this concentration of power; and it is theoretically possible that we could retain the benefits of complex organization while reducing the role of the state in providing a framework for organization. In practice, no one has yet accomplished this feat. Only the most remote and primitive peoples can do without the state. As soon as the modern world touches an area, the inhabitants must either form a state or take refuge in the shadow of an already existing one.

If we cannot escape from the state, it is of some importance to understand it. One way of understanding it is to study its history—to see how and when this form of organization came into existence, what needs it satisfied, on what principles it was based. A study of the origins of the modern European state may throw some light on the characteristics and problems of the state today. It may be especially helpful in illuminating differences among types of states, and in explaining why some states have better balanced or more effective types of organization than others.

4

We should perhaps begin with a definition of the state, but most attempts to make such a definition have not been very satisfactory. A state exists chiefly in the hearts and minds of its people; if they do not believe it is there, no logical exercise will bring it to life. States have flourished which meet none of the criteria of the political scientist, for example the Netherlands in the seventeenth century. Rather than definition, let us look for some of the signs which show us that a state is coming into existence. These signs will be especially useful for our enquiry, since we are concerned with origins and not with the final form of states.

The first sign is easy to recognize because it is purely external. A human community must persist in space and time if it is to become a state. Only by living and working together in a given area for many generations can a group of people develop the patterns of organization which are essential for statebuilding. Temporary coalitions of groups which have some common interests are not apt to be the nuclei of states unless the emergency which causes the coalition lasts so long or recurs so frequently that the coalition gradually becomes permanent, as it did, for example, in the case of the Franks. Even regular meetings and repeated alliances of groups which acknowledge a common origin will not suffice to form a state; the contacts must be continuous, not intermittent. The history of ancient Greece illustrates both these points; neither coalitions against Persia nor the Olympic Games ever made a single state out of the Greek cities. Geographically, there must be a core area within which the group can build its political system, though a certain amount of fluctuation along the fringes is permissible. States require permanent institutions, and it is difficult to establish such institutions if the area in which they are to be applied changes constantly, or if the cohesion of the group is greater at one season of the year than at another. This is why true nomads do not establish states;[1] a certain proportion of them must become sedentary before any high degree of political organization is possible. Even a non-nomadic people which leaves its old home—voluntarily or involuntarily—usually loses some of its political coherence and has to start the process of state-building afresh, as the history of the American West demonstrates.

With continuity in space and time the next sign of the possible emergence of a state appears: the formation of impersonal, relatively permanent political institutions. Primitive or temporary political groupings can function through personal, unstructured relationships, such as meetings of prominent men, or neighborhood assemblies. Even at this level certain customary ways of dealing with matters of general concern will develop; there will be procedures for settling internal disputes and for organizing armed groups in case of war. More than this is needed, however, if the community is to persist in time and retain its hold on a geographical area, if loosely linked neighborhoods are to be welded into an effective political unit, if more effective use is to be made of the varied resources and abilities of the people. There must be in-

[1] See Philip C. Salzman, "Political Organization among Nomadic Peoples," *Proceedings of the American Philosophical Society*, III (1967), 115-131, and references given in his bibliography.

stitutions which can survive changes in leadership and fluctuations in the degree of cooperation among sub-groups, institutions which allow a certain degree of specialization in political affairs and thus increase the efficiency of the political process, institutions which strengthen the sense of political identity of the group. When such institutions appear, a key point in state-building has been reached.

On the other hand, the appearance of specialized institutions does not inevitably lead to the creation of a state. The institutions may be developed simply to protect the private interests of the wealthy and the powerful. A tribal leader, for example, may wish to have a regular accounting of the income from his lands or his herds, just as any prudent property-owner would. Such an accounting does not necessarily lay the foundations of a Treasury Department. A group of aristocratic landholders may wish to reduce feuds which are damaging their properties or decimating their numbers, and so be led to create a system of law courts. As the early history of Iceland shows, the existence of such courts does not necessarily lead to the acceptance of the supremacy of law, nor to the emergence of an authority which will enforce the law. The courts may be only a convenience, to be used or not depending on the circumstances.

Nevertheless, precisely because in the pre-state era there can be no sharp distinction between public and private, any persisting institution may in time become part of a state structure though it was not originally intended to have this function. We have seen this happen in comparatively recent times. The Commonwealth of Massachusetts and the British Empire of

India grew out of the institutions of private corporations. One of the oldest public offices in the world today is that of the sheriff, but the earliest sheriffs were simply estate-managers of Anglo-Saxon kings.

A stronger objection to placing too much emphasis on permanent institutions is that institutions may be purely external devices by which a ruler (or ruling class) dominates a subject people. The existence of permanent institutions does not prove that subjects have accepted them as necessary, or that they have created the climate of opinion that is essential for the existence of the state. But persisting institutions are likely to produce a gradual change in attitudes. They may form a trellis on which the idea of the state can grow. Even colonial institutions which struck no deep roots among subject populations can and have been used as the skeleton of the structure of a new state.

More important than the existence of continuing institutions is evidence that they are growing in prestige and authority. For example, are there courts which can give final decisions that bind all the people in a given area and which cannot be reversed by any other authority? Medieval popes proclaimed that they "judged all and could be judged by none";[2] when were certain secular authorities able to make such a claim? In more general terms, when does the idea of

[2] This is the basic doctrine of the *Dictatus Papae* of 1075, articles 18-21. See the English translation in Ewart Lewis, *Medieval Political Ideas* (New York, 1954), II, 381: "that his decision ought to be reviewed by no one, and that he alone can review the decisions of everyone; that he ought to be judged by no one." Innocent III put it more compactly: he is the one "qui de omnibus judicat et a nemine judicatur." See R. W. and A. J. Carlyle, *A History of Mediaeval Political Theory* (Edinburgh, 1928), IV, 153.

sovereignty begin to emerge? It is harder to prove the existence of an idea than the existence of an institution, and the difficulty is compounded by the inadequacy of the European political vocabulary of early periods. Sovereignty existed in fact long before it could be described in theory (1300 AD as opposed to 1550).[3] It is also true that rulers who claimed what was in effect sovereign power were not always able to make their claims good. But the turning point was the recognition of the need for a final authority, not the possession of a "monopoly of power." As long as most of the politically active population admitted that there should be an authority capable of making final decisions, a good many violations of the principle could be tolerated in practice.

This leads to the final, most important, and most nebulous of our tests: a shift in loyalty from family, local community, or religious organization to the state and the acquisition by the state of a moral authority to back up its institutional structure and its theoretical legal supremacy. At the end of the process, subjects accept the idea that the interests of the state must prevail, that the preservation of the state is the highest social good. But the change is usually so gradual that the process is hard to document; it is impossible to say

[3] On this problem see Gaines Post, *Studies in Medieval Legal Thought* (Princeton, 1964), chs. 5, 8, 10, and esp. pp. 280-289, 301-309, 445-453, 463-478; E. H. Kantorowicz, *The King's Two Bodies* (Princeton, 1957), ch. 5, esp. pp. 236-258. Note that the Statute of Westminster I (1275) c. 17, says that even in Wales, where the king's writ does not run, the king as sovereign can do justice to all, and that Beaumanoir, writing in France about the same time, says in his *Coutumes de Beauvaisis*, para. 1043, that the king is sovereign over all, that he can make such laws ("establissemens") as please him for the common good, and that everyone is subject to his justice.

9

that at a certain point on the time scale loyalty to the state becomes the dominant loyalty. The problem is complicated by the fact that loyalty to the state is not the same thing as nationalism; in fact, in some areas nationalism worked against loyalty to existing states. Even in the fortunate countries where nationalism eventually reinforced loyalty to the state, loyalty to the state came first and was a much cooler kind of emotion. It had about the same temperature as humanitarianism, and it was, in some ways, a kind of humanitarianism. The state gave greater peace and security, more opportunity for the good life, than loose associations of communities; therefore it should be supported.

To sum up this part of the discussion, what we are looking for is the appearance of political units persisting in time and fixed in space, the development of permanent, impersonal institutions, agreement on the need for an authority which can give final judgments, and acceptance of the idea that this authority should receive the basic loyalty of its subjects. We shall be seeking evidence of these changes in Western Europe in the period 1100 to 1600. This is not because there were no states in earlier periods, or in the non-European world—certainly the Greek *polis* was a state, the Han Empire of China was a state, the Roman Empire was a state. But we are looking for the origins of the modern state, and the modern state did not derive directly from any of these early examples. The men who laid the foundations for the first European states knew nothing of East Asia and were far removed in time from Greece and Rome. While they learned something from Rome through the study of

Roman law, and something from Greece through hints in Aristotelian treatises, basically they had to reinvent the state by their own efforts. And the type of state they invented proved more successful than most of the earlier models. In the ancient world, states tended to fall into two classes: the great, imperfectly integrated empires, and the small, but highly cohesive units such as the Greek city-state. Each type had weaknesses. The empires were militarily strong, but could enlist only a small proportion of their inhabitants in the political process or, indeed, in any activity that transcended immediate local interests. This meant a considerable waste of human resources; it also meant that loyalty to the state was lukewarm. The vast majority of the subjects of an empire did not believe that the preservation of the state was the highest social good; in case after case they viewed the collapse of empires with equanimity, and either reverted to smaller political units or accepted without protest incorporation in a new empire ruled by a new elite. The city-state made far more effective use of its inhabitants than the empire; all citizens participated actively in the political process and in associated community activities. Loyalty to the state was strong; at times it approached the intensity of modern nationalism. But no city-state ever solved the problem of incorporating new territories and new populations into its existing structure, of involving really large numbers of people in its political life. Either the city-state became the nucleus of an empire (as Rome did) and so became subject to the ills of empire, or it remained small, militarily weak, and sooner or later the victim of conquest.

11

The European states which emerged after 1100 combined, to some extent, the strengths of both the empires and the city-states. They were large enough and powerful enough to have excellent chances for survival—some of them are approaching the thousand-year mark, which is a respectable age for any human organization. At the same time they managed to get a large proportion of their people involved in, or at least concerned with the political process, and they succeeded in creating some sense of common identity among local communities. They got more out of their people, both in the way of political and social activity and in loyalty than the ancient empires had done, even if they fell short of the full participation which had marked a city such as Athens.

The distinction between large, imperfectly integrated empires and small but cohesive political units applies fairly well to the Middle East, Central Asia, and India. It fits China (and eventually Japan) less well. But the ability of the European type of state to gain economic and political superiority proved so great that in the end it made the Chinese (or other non-European) experience seem irrelevant. The European model of the state became the fashionable model. No European state imitated a non-European model, but the non-European states either imitated the European model in order to survive or else went through a colonial experience which introduced large elements of the European system. The modern state, wherever we find it today, is based on the pattern which emerged in Europe in the period 1100 to 1600.

The Europeans, as was said earlier, had to reinvent the state by their own efforts, and for many centuries after the fall of the Roman Empire in the West it did not seem at all likely that they would succeed in this task. The Roman idea of the state was quickly forgotten in the troubled period of invasions and migrations; even the leaders of the Church, who preserved many Roman traditions, could not express the concept with any clarity. In the early Middle Ages the dominant form of political organization in Western Europe was the Germanic kingdom, and the Germanic kingdom was in some ways the complete antithesis of a modern state. It was based on loyalties to persons, not to abstract concepts or impersonal institutions. A kingdom was made up of the people who recognized a certain man as king, or, in the more stable societies, of the people who recognized a certain family as having a hereditary claim to leadership. These kingdoms lacked continuity in time and stability in space. Some were so ephemeral that we can describe them only by the name of a ruler, for example, the "kingdom of Samo" which flourished briefly in eastern Germany.[4] Some, which lasted longer in time, moved about fantastically in space; in a few generations the kingdom of the West Goths jumped from the region of the Baltic to that of the Black Sea to that of the Bay of Biscay. No regularly functioning institutions nor premonitions of sovereignty can be found in such a society. The king existed to deal with emergencies, not to head a legal or administrative system. He spoke for his people with the gods; he led them in battle against other kings, but each local community settled its own internal affairs. Security came from

[4] On Samo see J. Peisker in *Cambridge Medieval History* (Cambridge, Eng., 1926), II, 451-452.

family, and neighborhood, and lord, not from the king.

The Frankish kingdom of the eighth and ninth centuries, and the Anglo-Saxon kingdom of the tenth and eleventh centuries rose somewhat above this level. Each kingdom had established itself in a fixed area and had endured a respectable length of time. In each kingdom the king had accepted general responsibility for preserving peace and doing justice, and had created a uniform system of local courts to meet this responsibility.[5] But these steps toward state-building were premature; the basic social and economic structures could not bear the weight of even slightly centralized political institutions. Interests and loyalties were primarily local, limited to the family, the neighborhood, the county. Royal officials—dukes, counts and *vassi dominici* in Frankland, earls and thegns in England—tended to become leaders of autonomous local communities rather than agents of central authority. In Frankland the counts and dukes had become practically independent by 900, but their own authority in turn was being eroded by viscounts, castellans, and other leaders of smaller communities. This fragmentation of political power is one of the aspects of early feudalism. In fact feudalism is apt to appear whenever the strain of preserving a relatively large political unit proves to be beyond the economic and psychic resources of a society. And early feudalism can relieve the strain only by simplifying institutions and personalizing loyalties. It must start by working

[5] For England, see F. M. Stenton, *Anglo-Saxon England* (Oxford, 1943), pp. 289-296, 389, 485-495, 538-539, and J.E.A. Jolliffe, *Constitutional History of Medieval England* (London, 1937), pp. 57-74, 107-127; for France, F. L. Ganshof, *Frankish Institutions under Charlemagne* (Providence, 1968), pp. 71-97.

against state-building, even if in the end it can become a basis for state-building.

Fragmentation proceeded at different rates and to different degrees in each part of the old Frankish realm, but it went so far that by the year 1000 it would have been difficult to find anything like a state anywhere on the continent of Europe (except for the Byzantine Empire). England, united later than Frankland, naturally began to show signs of disintegration later. Twelfth-century England, left to its own devices, might have been as divided as eleventh-century France, but the Norman Conquest, by wiping out the old Anglo-Saxon aristocracy, eliminated one of the forces that was leading to fragmentation. There has been and will be endless speculation about the effects of the Conquest, but one thing is sure: by introducing a new, French-oriented ruling class, it erased much of the difference in timing between developments on the continent and developments in England. After 1066 the forces which encouraged or discouraged the emergence of the state in continental countries worked with equal effectiveness on England.

It is difficult to say what ideas and events revived the process of state-building in Western Europe in the late eleventh century. Certainly the spread of Christianity to unorthodox or heathen Germanic peoples and the improved organization of the Church were important. Western Europe was not really Christian until the end of the tenth century. Before that time many nominal Christians had little contact with the Church and one of the strongest of the Germanic groups—the Northmen—was not even nominally Christian. The Church already had many of the attributes of a state—for example, enduring institutions —and was developing others—for example, a theory of papal sovereignty.[6] The fact that churchmen were deeply involved in secular politics, that no ruler could function without their advice and assistance, meant that the political theories and the administrative techniques of the Church had a direct impact on lay government. The Church was also teaching that secular rulers were bound to give peace and justice to their subjects[7]—a doctrine which logically demanded the creation of new judicial and administrative institutions. But movement was slow; it was easier to admire the institutions of the Church than to imitate them, easier to admit royal responsibility for justice than to organize a judicial system. The influence of the Church, by itself, was not enough to create states.

Another, almost equally important factor, was the gradual stabilization of Europe, the ending of a long period of migration, invasion, and conquest. The early Germanic kings had destroyed the Empire in the West, but then they went on to destroy each other, with new invaders coming along to help the process. The Franks conquered rival kingdoms in Gaul and Germany only to find themselves split by civil war and shaken by attacks of the Northmen. The Ostrogoths and the Vandals were wiped out by the Eastern Empire, the Visigoths by a Moslem invasion. The Danes put an end to most of the Anglo-Saxon kingdoms. Only in the tenth century did the sole survivor, the kingdom of

---

[6] W. Ullmann, *The Growth of Papal Government in the Middle Ages* (London, 1955), pp. 276-299, 414-437.

[7] Kantorowicz, *The King's Two Bodies*, pp. 93-97; Carlyle, *History of Political Theory*, II, Part II, chs. 3, 5, 8.

Wessex, gain control of most of England. But after 1000 such sweeping changes became rare. The chief surviving kingdoms, the kingdom of England, the kingdom of the West Franks (which was to become France), and the kingdom of the East Franks (the nucleus of Germany), were to endure in one form or another down to our own day. The same thing happened at the local level; the great noble families took root in specific places instead of wandering about seeking power or plunder. No longer could a count from the Rhineland become ruler of western France, as the ancestor of the Capetians had done; no longer could a Viking leader make himself master of a French province as Rollo had done in Normandy.

This increased political stability created one of the essential conditions for state-building, continuity in space and time. Merely by enduring, some kingdoms and principalities began to acquire solidity. Certain peoples, occupying certain areas, remained for centuries in the same political grouping. A kingdom which had existed for generations was expected to continue to exist; it had become an accepted part of the political landscape. And the rulers of kingdoms or principalities which persisted in space and in time had opportunities and incentives to develop permanent institutions. If only for selfish reasons, they wanted internal security and some sort of organized connection between local communities and their own courts. Greater security and tighter controls would almost certainly increase the ruler's income, add to his prestige, and improve the chances that he could transmit his power and his possessions to his heirs. The desires of rulers coincided with the needs of their subjects. In an age of violence most men sought, above everything else, peace and security. There were pressures at all levels to strengthen weak governments so that they could perform their minimum duties of defense against internal and external disturbers of the peace. Thus in any political unit where there was some stability and continuity, one could expect that there would be efforts to create judicial institutions which would improve internal security and financial institutions which would provide the revenues necessary for defense against external enemies.

Curiously enough, the drive towards improved judicial and financial institutions was especially strong in some of the larger feudal lordships. Feudalism had destroyed the Frankish Empire, but it had not destroyed some of the socio-political changes wrought by that Empire. Even the most primitive feudal lordship was a more sophisticated political unit than a primitive Germanic tribe. Those who played political roles were clearly separated from the rest of the community. The political structure was an artificial creation—for example, the county, the office of count, the county court—and the political structure could be changed by deliberately planned acts—for example, the transfer of a court or of part of the jurisdiction of a court from one lord to another. Government was something separate from the folk-ways of the community, and a realization of this separateness was an essential ingredient in state-building. Moreover, feudalism had removed the strain of trying to preserve unviable political units and had thus created a more propitious climate of opinion for political experimentation. The effective unit of feudal government corresponded fairly well with the effective social and economic unit; the subjects of the same lord usually had a good deal in common. In many feudal principalities a strong feeling of loyalty to the lord developed, something which had been lacking in both the Later Roman Empire and in many of the Germanic kingdoms. Finally, the feudal lord, like other rulers, had strong incentives to try to improve his methods of government: the desire for more income and greater security for himself and his heirs. Thus in some areas, notably northern France, the more competent feudal lords took some of the first steps in state-building.

By modern standards one could not say that there was a notable increase in stability and security in the period following the year 1000. In contrast with earlier conditions, however, the improvement is undeniable; it was great enough to touch off an impressive revival in most parts of western Europe. Agricultural production increased; long-distance commerce increased; the population grew; men became more concerned about both religion and politics. It was not always easy to harmonize all these interests; it was especially difficult to mesh together the desire for more and better government with the desire for a reformed Church and a more Christian way of life. An early example will illustrate the point. The Peace Movement began in the troubled regions of central France in the tenth century as an attempt by the Church to organize peasants and other non-combatants into a sort of vigilante association to repress the violence and pillaging of feudal lords.[8] It was not very successful be-

---

[8] L. Hubert, *Studien zur Rechtsgeschichte der Gottesfrieden und Landesfrieden* (Ansbach, 1892); Georges Molinié, *L'organ-*

cause the lords were usually militarily superior to the untrained, poorly equipped armies of the Peace Associations. The Movement was also viewed with some suspicion by laymen, and even by conservative churchmen, because it involved the Church in the very secular business of war and criminal justice. But when the idea was taken up by powerful lords such as the duke of Normandy, when the Church was willing to take a secondary role and merely sanction the efforts of a lay ruler, then the Peace Movement proved useful. It gave dukes and counts an excuse for intervening in local affairs and for repressing acts of violence which threatened political stability.[9]

In the long run, churchmen and laymen were usually able to agree on methods to decrease the incidence of violence. But during the eleventh century they increasingly disagreed on a more fundamental question: the relationship between secular and religious authority. The two had been thoroughly intermingled in earlier centuries. Kings had been considered semi-religious personages and had had extensive influence in Church affairs. They appointed abbots, bishops, and often popes; they even intervened (as Charlemagne had) in matters of doctrine.[10] Lead-

ization judiciaire, militaire et financière des associations de la paix (Toulouse, 1912); L. C. Mackinney, "The People and Public Opinion in the Eleventh Century Peace Movement," *Speculum*, v (1930), 181-206; Hartmut Hoffman, *Gottesfriede und Truga Dei* (Stuttgart, 1964).

[9] For Normandy, see H. Prentout, "La trêve de Dieu en Normandie," *Mémoires de l'Académie de Caen*, n.s. vi (1931), 1-32; J. Yver, "L'interdiction de la guerre privée en Normandie," *Travaux de la semaine d'histoire de droit normand 1927* (Caen, 1928), pp. 307-348.

[10] Kantorowicz, *The King's Two Bodies*, ch. 3; J. W. Thompson, *Feudal Germany* (Chicago, 1928), chs. 1, 2; E. Amann

ing churchmen, on the other hand, played an important role in secular affairs, as advisers to kings, as administrators, as rulers of ecclesiastical principalities. The new leadership which grew up in the Church in the eleventh century at first sought only reform of the clergy. But it gradually became apparent that to reform the clergy the Church needed to be more independent of lay authority, and that to gain and preserve its independence the Church had to be centralized under the headship of the pope. A reformed and strongly centralized Church was bound to have wide influence in secular affairs. Some reformers thought that it should have final authority in all problems of social and political relationships. If Europe was to be really Christian, then it must have Christian leadership.[11]

This program, most forcefully expressed by Pope Gregory VII (1073-1085), destroyed essential parts of the earlier political structure of Europe. Lay rulers resisted the claims of the Church and the resulting struggle (the Investiture Conflict) lasted for almost half a century. During the quarrel the old symbiosis of religious and secular authorities was seriously weakened. Kings lost their semi-ecclesiastical character and some of their control over Church appointments. The Church gained leadership, if not complete control, of European society. The Church had separated itself sharply from secular political authorities; it was in-

---

and A. Dumas, *L'Église au pouvoir des laïques 888-1057* (Paris, 1948), Book I, ch. 2, Book II, chs. 2, 3, Book III, ch. 1.
[11] Gerd Tellenbach, *Church, State and Christian Society at the Time of the Investiture Conflict* (Oxford, 1940), pp. 147-161; Ullmann, *Growth of Papal Government*, pp. 272-299; A. Fliche, *La réforme grégorienne* (Paris, 1946), pp. 55-64, 76-83.

dependent at the highest level, and was thus able to assert a considerable amount of autonomy at lower levels. The Gregorian reformers had won a victory, even if it was a partial victory.[12]

Like all victories, the victory of the Church in the Investiture Conflict had unforeseen consequences. By asserting its unique character, by separating itself so clearly from lay governments, the Church unwittingly sharpened concepts about the nature of secular authority. Definitions and arguments might vary, but the most ardent Gregorian had to admit that the Church could not perform all political functions, that lay rulers were necessary and had a sphere in which they should operate. They might be subject to the guidance and correction of the Church, but they were not a part of the administrative structure of the Church. They headed another kind of organization, for which there was as yet no generic term. In short, the Gregorian concept of the Church almost demanded the invention of the concept of the State. It demanded it so strongly that modern writers find it exceedingly difficult to avoid describing the Investiture Conflict as a struggle of Church and State.

To yield to this temptation would be erroneous, but the reorganization of the political structure of Europe during and after the Conflict did prepare the way for the emergence of the state. For one thing, the claims of the revived Western Empire to universal domination could no longer be taken seriously. When Church and Empire cooperated closely, as they had under

[12] Besides the books mentioned in note 11, see G. Barraclough, *The Origins of Modern Germany* (Oxford, 1949), pp. 127-155; and N. Cantor, *Church, Kingship and Lay Investiture in England* (Princeton, 1958), chs. 1, 5.

Charlemagne and the Ottos, imperial supremacy could be admitted, at least in theory; but the Investiture Conflict weakened the Empire more than any other secular political organization. Other rulers settled their disputes with the reformers independently and on better terms than did the emperor. Western Europe might be a religious unit, but it was clearly not a political unit. Each kingdom or principality had to be treated as a separate entity; the foundations for a multi-state system had been laid.

At the same time the Investiture Conflict reinforced a tendency which already existed: the tendency to consider the lay ruler primarily as a guarantor and a distributor of justice. The Gregorian reformers might believe that the Church defined what justice was, but even they admitted that in normal conditions it was the duty of secular rulers to see that justice was dispensed to the people. It was even more important for kings to emphasize this function. If they no longer shared responsibility for the guidance and governance of the Church, if they were no longer "bishops for external affairs," then their only excuse for existence was to enforce justice. But if they were to enforce justice, then codes of law must be developed and judicial institutions improved. Both these steps, of course, are helpful in state-building, but they do not always come as early nor do they always have the importance which they did in Western Europe.

The fact that there was such a strong emphasis on law at the very beginning of Western European states was to have a profound influence on their future development. The state was based on law and existed to enforce law. The ruler was bound morally (and often politically) by the law, and European law was not merely criminal law, as was that of many other regions; it regulated family and business relationships, and the possession and the use of property. In no other political system was law so important; in no other society were lawyers to play such an important role. European states did not always attain their ideal of being primarily law-states, but that this was their ideal was an important factor in gaining the loyalty and support of their subjects.

Perhaps the latest of the stimuli which led to the emergence of the European state was the rapid growth in the number of educated men during the twelfth century.[13] It is difficult to create permanent, impersonal institutions without written records and official documents. In fact, the written document is the best guarantee of permanence and the best insulator between an administrator and personal pressures, which is precisely why citizens who want rules twisted in their favor always go behind the written document to the person who can quash it. In the early twelfth century the number of men who could prepare records and documents was limited, and institutional development was equally limited. But part of the general European revival was a tremendous increase in the desire for learning; thousands of young men flocked to the schools and then took service with lay or ecclesiastical officials. By the end of the twelfth century the shortage of clerks and account-

---

[13] C. H. Haskins, *Renaissance of the Twelfth Century* (Cambridge, Mass., 1927); G. Paré, A. Brunet, P. Tremblay, *La renaissance du XIIe siècle* (Paris, 1933); D. Knowles, *The Evolution of Medieval Thought* (London, 1962), pp. 71-171; R. W. Southern, *The Making of the Middle Ages*, ch. 4.

ants was almost overcome; by the end of the thirteenth century there was probably a surplus of men who could do this kind of work

One type of education needs special mention: the study of law. Most young men took only the course in arts, which emphasized correct use of language and logic. Of those who went on to higher studies, by far the largest number enrolled in the schools of law. They studied canon law, Roman law (as found in the *Corpus Iuris Civilis* of Justinian), or both. Teachers in these schools were famous throughout Europe and their students gained high positions, especially in the Church. Nevertheless, the influence of the academic study of law should not be exaggerated. The first state-building institutions were already in existence before the law schools had begun to function, and Roman law was of little immediate use in most of Europe north of the Alps. England, Germany, and northern France used customary law, which was not taught in the schools; and men skilled in customary law could achieve remarkable results with little or no knowledge of Roman law. What was important about the study of Roman law was that it furnished a set of categories into which new ideas could be fitted and a vocabulary by which they could be described. Thus the Roman idea of a distinction between civil and criminal law was helpful to English judges who were trying to write textbooks on the rapidly developing English common law.[14] The idea of public welfare and the duty of the ruler to enhance the public welfare was

[14] Glanvill, *De Legibus et Consuetudines Regni Angliae*, ed. G. E. Woodbine (New Haven, 1932); written in 1187, he begins his substantive discussion with the statement: "Placitorum aliud criminale aliud civile" (p. 42).

25

useful in justifying innovations such as general taxation.[15] The Romans did not have a word which was exactly the equivalent of our "state," but their "respublica" or "commonwealth" was fairly close and formed a nucleus around which ideas of the state could crystallize. But all of this would have been purely abstract learning if Western Europe had not already started the process of creating legal institutions. It was because they already had civil law, taxes, and even a vague idea of the state that thirteenth-century Europeans could use and understand the Roman parallels. The existence of those parallels certainly helped to sharpen the definitions and clarify the thinking of judges and administrators. The fact that discussions of political theory were often expressed in terms of Roman law reinforced the already existing tendency to use law as the basis and justification for the creation of states. But while the revival of Roman law facilitated and perhaps accelerated the process of state-building, it was certainly not the primary cause and probably not even a necessary condition.

The discussion of the influence of Roman law has led us far past our original starting-point. Let us return to the early twelfth century and examine the political structures which were then emerging. We can begin with an important generalization: the first permanent institutions in Western Europe dealt with internal and not external affairs. High courts of justice and Treasury Departments existed long before Foreign Offices and Departments of Defense. This priority of internal institutions was helpful in several ways.

[15] Post, *Studies*, pp. 258-290.

It fitted better with the dominant secular ideals of justice and the rule of law, which were easy to apply to internal problems and very difficult to apply in external affairs. There were obvious advantages to everyone in building an effective system of courts; it was harder to demonstrate the value of a standing army. Finally, there was less pressure on scarce human resources if the most competent and intelligent officials could be allowed to specialize, for the most part, in internal affairs. By way of contrast, consider the plight of a newly created state today, which may have to use its most capable people as diplomats or army officers.

The reasons for this concentration on internal affairs are obvious. The fragmented condition of Europe and the weakness of its political units did not permit any sustained or long-range activity in external affairs. No ruler could raise an army of more than a few thousand men, nor could he keep such an army in being more than a few months. Standing armies or permanent officer corps were unthinkable. Most rulers were concerned only about relations with their immediate neighbors; England had little to do with Aragon or France with Sweden. Even between neighbors the issues were more apt to be settled by raids and reprisals than by diplomacy, and truces and peaces could be handled on an ad hoc basis. In a Europe without states and without boundaries the concept of "foreign affairs" had no meaning, and so no machinery for dealing with foreign affairs was needed.

Conversely, precisely because the political system of Europe was so weak and fragmented, rulers who wanted to preserve their status and hand it on to their sons had to make some effort to form coherent political units out of the scattered lands and rights of government which they possessed. This meant, first and foremost, improving the art of estate management. With general taxes almost unknown, the income of kings and princes came almost entirely from their lands, their tolls and market dues, and their share of fines imposed for certain offenses in certain courts.[16] But since the lands were never contiguous and tolls and rights of justice were shared with members of the aristocracy, it was difficult for a king to know exactly what he should receive and almost as difficult to collect what was due even when the amount was known. The first permanent functionaries were estate-managers—the reeves and shire-reeves (sheriffs) of England, the *prévôts* of France, the ministerials of Germany. They centralized the scattered revenues of their territories and made them available to their masters. In doing this, they had to keep some sort of records and subject themselves to some sort of accounting. This development took place much more rapidly in England than elsewhere, but in most countries central

[16] Even in the 12th century, when state-building had already begun, and even in the most advanced political units, such as England, Normandy, and Flanders, revenues were largely of the type mentioned in the text. See B. Lyon and A. E. Verhulst, *Medieval Finance* (Providence, 1967); L. Delisle, "Des revenues publics en Normandie au XIIᵉ et XIIIᵉ siècles," *Bibliothèque de l'École des Chartes* x, xi, xii (1848-1849, 1852); *Magnum rotulum, 31 Henry I*, ed. J. Hunter (London, 1833): royal revenue in England in 1130. France was still in this state in 1202; see F. Lot and R. Fawtier, *Le premier budget de la monarchie française: Le compte général de 1202-1203* (Paris, 1932).

financial institutions grew out of the work of local estate-managers.

Profits of justice were an appreciable part of local revenues (since the usual penalty for most misdeeds was a fine), and it was part of the duty of local agents of government to hold the courts which produced such revenues. This was satisfactory as long as courts dealt mainly with squabbles among peasants and as long as the fines imposed were fixed, and usually rather small sums. The connection between the administration of justice and the collection of revenue remained close throughout the Middle Ages. Even when specialized groups of judges appeared, the judges were often used as revenue collectors[17] and the old revenue collectors (sheriffs, *prévôts*, and the like) continued to hold courts for petty offenses. Nevertheless, rulers gradually began to see that justice was something more than a source of revenue. It was a way of asserting the authority and increasing the power of the king or greater lords. Therefore, the ablest rulers tried to increase the number of cases that came to their courts.

There were several devices by which the jurisdiction of a court could be increased. Serious criminal offenses, such as murder, could be reserved for the court of the king (or a duke or a count). The reservation of these cases (called pleas of the crown or pleas of the sword) allowed the ruler to intervene in districts where he had no lands and no local rights of justice.[18] In civil cases, special procedures could be

[17] W. Stubbs, *Select Charters* (Oxford, 1921), pp. 251-257. English circuit judges in 1194 are to hear all pleas; they are also to inquire about escheats, wardships, and other profitable royal rights and are told to tallage the king's towns.

[18] Glanvill, *De Legibus*, p. 42, chs. 1, 2; *Le très ancien cou-*

developed by which litigants could by-pass the court of the local lord and go directly to a royal (ducal, comital) court. These procedures were usually based on the twin ideas of keeping the peace and protecting possession. Since disturbing possession without due legal process was apt to cause disorder, the superior could intervene and issue a court order to preserve or restore the status quo.[19] Theoretically the lower (baronial) court still had jurisdiction; actually the order of the superior court usually settled the case. Thus rear-vassals could be protected against their immediate lords by the king (duke, count), and their primary loyalty began to go to the man who protected them. Finally, it was the duty of a king to see that justice was done throughout his realm. If a lower court made an unjust decision, the only way to remedy the injustice was to allow an appeal to the court of the suzerain. A lord whose decisions could be overruled was a lord who had lost much of his authority.[20]

These devices were used in varying degrees by the men who were building states in the twelfth and thir-

---

tumier de Normandie, texte Latin, ed. E. J. Tardif (Rouen, 1881), p. 43, ch. 53: "de placitis ensis ad Ducem pertinentibus"; E. Perrot, *Les cas royaux* (Paris, 1910).

[19] This is the protection of seisin, a basic idea in the English common law; see F. Pollock and F. W. Maitland, *History of English Law* (Cambridge, Eng., 1923), i, 145-149. It also was important in France; see L. Buisson, *König Ludwig IX, der Heilige, und das Recht* (Freiburg, 1954), pp. 10-19, 99-118.

[20] Appeals were especially important in building the French state; see F. Lot and R. Fawtier, *Histoire des institutions françaises au Moyen Age,* Vol. ii, *Institutions Royales* (Paris, 1958), pp. 296-323. A thirteenth-century lawyer, Philippe de Beaumanoir, stated the rule clearly in his *Coutumes de Beauvaisis* (ed. A. Salmon, Paris, 1899), para. no. 1043: "Et si n'i a nul si grant dessous li [the king] qui ne puist estre tres en sa court pour defaute de droit ou pour faus jugement et pour tous les cas qui touchent le roi."

teenth centuries. Direct intervention by the king was more widespread in England than in France; appeals to the royal court from a baronial court were much more common in France than in England. But whatever the emphasis, in each country the theoretical supremacy of the king became a little more real every decade, and the distinction between districts ruled directly by the king and those held of him by the barons became a little less important. When the process reached its natural conclusion, the political geography of a kingdom (or a principality) was drastically altered. Instead of scattered islands of political power, each almost isolated from the other, there was a solid block of territory in which one ruler had final authority. It took centuries to attain this result, but even the early steps in building a judicial system greatly improved the position of the heads of newly developing states. Lords seeking independence could succeed only by increasing their military and economic resources, and such gains could usually be achieved only through violence to neighbors and unprecedented demands on subordinates. If a superior court could prevent local wars by enforcing peaceful solutions of quarrels and if it could keep a lord from unduly exploiting his men, then the establishment of a new, autonomous principality would become more difficult.

On the whole, the climate of opinion favored this development of effective courts of law. As we have already seen, the Church insisted that justice was the essential attribute of secular rulers. Kings promised in their coronation oaths to do justice, and political theorists argued that an unjust king was no king at all, but a tyrant.[21] Kings were quite ready to accept the idea that justice was all-important, since it was a sign of their authority and a weapon by which they might achieve supremacy in their realms. For the common folk, and even for many members of the lesser aristocracy, justice meant protection against violence and loss of lands. Thus rulers who tried to create regularly functioning law courts were assured of almost universal approval. The most warlike barons could not object to the existence of courts, though they might be very slow to obey their orders.

For all these reasons, permanent judicial institutions were developed almost as early as permanent financial institutions. The institutions were somewhat more specialized than the personnel. The same man might be both judge and revenue collector, but when he acted as judge he followed certain procedures and formalities which he did not have to follow when he was simply collecting rents. And as time went on, the law administered in the courts became better defined, more complicated, and more difficult to expound without special training. By 1200 men were writing treatises on the customary law of England and Normandy;[22] by 1250 they were relying on past precedents as a guide to their decisions.[23] The competence

[21] Carlyle, *History of Political Theory*, II, 125-140. On coronation oaths, see the articles of P. E. Schramm, which are now being collected in *Kaiser, Könige und Päpste*. Band II (Stuttgart, 1968), pp. 99-257 contains his studies on coronation orders down to the early 10th century, and Band III will include several more.

[22] Glanvill in England, see note 14; the unknown author of the *Très ancien coutumier* in Normandy, see note 18.

[23] *Bracton's Note Book*, ed. F. W. Maitland, 3 vols. (London, 1887), is a collection of notes on earlier cases used by a

and the procedure of courts were more sharply defined by each succeeding generation of legal experts. By 1300 there were men who devoted almost all of their time to the law; the judges of the central courts of England under Edward I were as highly trained in the English common law as any professor at Bologna was trained in Roman law. The two pillars of the medieval state were the Treasury and the High Court; by the end of the thirteenth century both institutions were manned by experienced, professionally minded officials.

Not all the professional personnel of a twelfth- or thirteenth-century government were used for estate management, local administration, and the administration of justice. There had to be a central office to coordinate the work of the men charged with special duties, an office that issued orders to revenue collectors and judges, an office that could deal directly with the prelates and barons who still had considerable responsibilities for maintaining internal order and security against external threats. This office, the chancery, was also charged with all the work that had not yet been delegated to organized departments, such as correspondence with the pope and with foreign princes. The head of the office, the chancellor, was, in Stubbs' phrase, a secretary of state for all departments.[24] He was always a high ranking cleric, by the thirteenth century usually a bishop, but he often had had experience in lesser positions in the government. Even if the chancellor had had no professional ex-

famous 13th-century English judge, who wrote a great treatise on English law.

[24] W. Stubbs, *Constitutional History of England* (Oxford, 1891), I, 381.

perience, the men who worked in his office were expert clerks who developed and preserved regular administrative routines and carefully worded, consistent formulae for their letters. Chancery clerks played an essential role in the development of medieval states. Central administration depended on the diligence with which they did their work and the precision with which they formulated their orders and instructions. The twelfth century saw a notable advance in the professional skill of most chanceries. Vague and general phrases were replaced by specific forms of wording which could not be misunderstood. The papal chancery was far in advance and served to some extent as a model for others, but by the time of Henry II (1154-1189) the English chancery was not far behind. France lagged a little behind England, but was showing unmistakable signs of improvement.[25] By the thirteenth century almost every European government had an effective chancery.

Thus in the centuries between 1000 and 1300 some of the essential elements of the modern state began to appear. Political entities, each with its own basic core of people and lands, gained legitimacy by enduring through generations. Permanent institutions for financial and judicial business were established. Groups of professional administrators were developed. A central coordinating agency, the chancery, had emerged with a staff of highly trained clerks. These professional ad-

[25] A. Giry, *Manuel de diplomatique* (Paris, 1925), pp. 661-704, 731-764, for the papal and Capetian chanceries. For England, see L. Delisle's Introduction to his *Recueil des actes de Henri II* (Paris, 1916), especially pp. 1 and 151. Though the *Recueil* includes only acts dealing with Henry's French possessions, the remarks about the chancery apply to England as well.

ministrators were not as yet very numerous, and they therefore could not be highly specialized. They had to be assisted by short-term or part-time agents— clerks whose main career was going to be in the Church, minor barons and knights, or wealthy burgesses. Many of these men were willing to work a few years, or part of the time each year, as estate-managers, financial agents, local administrators, or judges. In this way they could gain royal favor and increased income, even if they did not plan to serve the government permanently. But everywhere there were men who spent most of their lives as professional administrators, and their number increased markedly in the thirteenth century.

These basic elements of the state appeared almost everywhere in Western Europe during the twelfth and thirteenth centuries. But while they appeared everywhere, their rate of growth was uneven. The rate was most rapid in England, France, and the Spanish kingdoms; much less rapid in Germany; rapid, but distorted in Italy. The Spanish kingdoms, occupied with their own particular problem of the conquest and assimilation of Moorish territories, had little influence on the institutions of the rest of Europe until the end of the fifteenth century. The Germans failed to build large and enduring states; their typical political unit was the principality, and in the institutions of their principalities they imitated rather than innovated. In Italy the brilliant promise of the twelfth-century kingdom of Sicily failed to survive the misfortunes and the political blunders of the thirteenth century. The most successful political organizations in Italy after 1300 were the city-states; but the city-states did not face the same problems as the great kingdoms, and much of their experience was inapplicable north of the Alps. Thus England and France developed the most influential models of the European state; their political ideas and institutions were imitated more widely than those of any other European country. Their example was particularly important in the crucial period of the late thirteenth and early fourteenth centuries: the period in which the concept (if not the word) of sovereignty appeared; the period in which basic loyalty definitely shifted from Church, community, and family to the emerging state. It is therefore desirable to examine in some detail the process of state-building in England and in France between 1100 and 1300.

English rulers had less difficulty than their French cousins in achieving internal sovereignty. England was a small kingdom, not much larger than some of the great duchies of France or Germany. An active king could visit most parts of his realm with some regularity. Moreover, a long series of conquests had prevented the rise of strong provincial rulers or the development of deeply entrenched provincial institutions. Danish invasions wiped out all the old Anglo-Saxon dynasties except the House of Wessex. The slow reconquest of central and northern England by the kings of Wessex in its turn wiped out the Danish ruling families. Each region preserved its own customs, but there was no king of Kent, of Mercia, or of the Danelaw to build enduring institutions on the basis of these differing customs. Such institutions as existed were uniform throughout the country—the shire-court, the hundred-court, the borough-court. Local officials—

aldermen (earls) and reeves—represented the interests of the king rather than those of local communities. And when, as a result of the second Danish conquest of the eleventh century, certain great families began to take root in some shires, they were soon uprooted by William the Conqueror. While William gave extensive powers to the earls of certain frontier counties, these men were not able to establish powerful provincial dynasties; and most of his followers received not compact territorial units, but widely scattered grants of manors and rights of government. By 1100 it was clear that no earl or baron had a sufficient concentration of land or power to create an autonomous provincial administration. If England was going to have permanent institutions they would be royal institutions.

Here again England was fortunate. Because no areas had been monopolized by provincial dynasties the king still had lands and rights of justice in all parts of his realm. Because his lands and rights were so widely dispersed he had to have agents everywhere— sheriffs and bailiffs, keepers of castles and forests. Keeping track of the income produced by hundreds of different sources made plain the need for a central financial office. Seeing a need and doing something about it are, of course, two very different things, but the last Anglo-Saxon kings had developed important elements of a central accounting system. William and his sons carried this process much further. Early in the twelfth century the English Exchequer appeared: an institution which performed many functions but which had as its basic and most highly organized task the responsibility of auditing accounts submitted by royal officials from all parts of the realm. The Exchequer kept meticulously detailed records; it had a highly professional staff; it became so solidly established that it could function even in periods of civil war. If anything, it solidified a little prematurely. It was too bound by its own rules (it could spend ten pounds to recover a debt of ten pence), but it certainly was an enduring and unifying institution. Directly or indirectly, the work of the Exchequer touched everyone in England.[26]

The same historical circumstances help explain the rise of an all-pervasive system of royal courts. Not only did William inherit widespread rights of justice from his Anglo-Saxon predecessors; he also added immeasurably both to his problems and his powers by confiscating and redistributing most of the land in England. If all titles were based on grants or confirmations by the king, then it was natural that the king and his court would be asked to settle disputes over possession of land and the rights which went with land. "Court" is of course an ambiguous word; at first it meant no more than the great men—bishops, barons, and household officials—who were with the king. But even in the eleventh century some of these men were more apt to be called on to deal with legal problems than others, and during the twelfth century a group of royal justices appeared. The English king's court was busy—far busier than most of its contemporaries—and so it began to develop fixed rules and procedures for dealing with routine cases. Regular procedure

[26] On the Exchequer see R. L. Poole, *The Exchequer in the Twelfth Century* (Oxford, 1912); C. Johnson, *Dialogus de Scaccario: The Course of the Exchequer* (London, 1950); Lyon and Verhulst, *Medieval Finance*, pp. 57-71.

made the court more efficient, and more popular. By 1215 the barons of England thought that a permanent, central court of justice was essential for the good government of England.[27]

The central court, however, was at first only for great men and great cases. It could not take care of all disputes over land tenure; it was even less capable of dealing with the criminal cases—murder, arson, rape, robbery—which were reserved to the king throughout most of England. Yet justice was a source of revenue and a sign of power; it was to the king's advantage to have as many cases heard by his court as possible. The solution was to send out circuit judges —delegates of the central court—armed with new and efficacious procedures. The circuit judges could relieve overworked sheriffs of most of their judicial duties; they could also do work that could not be done by the courts of feudal barons. Baronial courts were weak and inefficient; they usually tried to compromise disputes and they were seldom able to give quick remedies to the dispossessed. Royal judges did not exactly compete with baronial courts; rather they took over areas in which the baronial courts were not operating. The new procedure of the royal courts was designed to cut down delay, to get quick, easily enforceable decisions in cases where decisions had been hard to reach. There was a deliberate attempt to reduce complicated problems to simple questions that could be answered by men with little knowledge of law or of remote events. Thus in cases involving land tenure the most common question was: "Who was last

[27] Magna Carta, article 17: "communia placita non sequantur curiam nostram sed teneantur in aliquo loco certo."

in peaceful possession?" not "Who has best title?" The question was answered by a group of neighbors, drawn from the law-abiding men of the district in which the property lay. They gave a collective response, based on their own knowledge and observations; there was no need for testimony and little opportunity for legal arguments. This procedure rapidly developed into trial by jury; the questions put to the jury became more diversified and more complicated until finally almost all disputes involving land or rights annexed to land could be settled by the verdict of a jury.

Juries were also used to collect accusations of crime. The neighborhood reported all cases of crime through its accusing (grand) jury; the men accused were arrested and tried by the circuit judges. Royal officials were somewhat slower to accept the verdict of a jury as conclusive in criminal cases than they had been in civil suits, naturally enough, since a mistake about possession of land could always be corrected while a death sentence could not. Nevertheless, by the middle of the thirteenth century, most criminal cases were begun by the accusation of a grand jury and settled by the verdict of a trial jury.

The use of juries made it possible for judges to hear many cases in a single day. Since there were seldom more than twenty judges, this was the only way to handle an increasing workload. The juries also helped to make the king's justice popular. Given the tight-knit character of rural communities, a jury of neighbors usually knew the facts in the case; this was an improvement on earlier, irrational procedures such as trial by battle or ordeals. Since the jury spoke for the whole community and gave a group verdict, it was less subject to pressure than individual witnesses would have been. Theoretically the Church's system (later adopted by French judges) of interrogating witnesses one by one was fairer. Actually, medieval men thought of litigation as merely a continuation of combat by other means, and witnesses were usually so partisan that it is doubtful that their testimony came any nearer the truth than the collective judgment of a jury of the neighborhood. In any case, knights, lesser landholders, and ordinary freemen in England found that the jury gave them some protection against the rich and the powerful. They flocked to the king's courts; by the thirteenth century all cases of any importance and many cases of no significance whatever were heard by the king's judges. The royal government had succeeded in involving almost the entire free population of the country in the work of the law courts, either as litigants or as jurors.[28]

A by-product of the development of the Exchequer and the royal law courts was to stimulate the growth of the chancery. Exact accounting required not only accurate reporting by sheriffs, but also a careful record and precise formulation of the orders that authorized the sheriffs to pay out certain sums or to receive credit for lands and rights alienated by the king. The English system of justice also depended heavily on the work of the chancery clerks. Each case had to begin with a writ issued by the chancery which defined the matters

[28] For the development of English courts in the 12th century, see Pollock and Maitland, *History of English Law*, I, 79-110, 136-173; W. S. Holdsworth, *History of English Law* (Boston, 1922), I, 32-54; T. F. Plucknett, *A Concise History of the Common Law* (Boston, 1956), pp. 101-113, 139-150.

in dispute and the procedure to be followed. English writs of the late twelfth century are admirable documents, terse, clear, and forceful. They could not be misunderstood and so there was less chance of their being disobeyed.

More generally, all branches of the English government were keeping careful records by the end of the twelfth century. The Exchequer preserved the reports of the sheriffs; the judges kept records of their decisions; the chancery had registers of the letters it sent out. The abundance of written records solidified rapidly growing institutions. There were ready-made formulae for almost every occasion, which saved a great deal of time, and left top administrators free to deal with abnormal problems. Precedents were easy to find, so that governmental action was consistent and predictable. In fact, English institutions were so well established that the government could run itself without much direction from the throne, as was shown during the ten-year reign of Richard I (1189-1199) when the king was in the country for only a few months.

England by 1200 had permanent institutions run by professional or semi-professional officials. It had also seen two actions which later on would have been considered assertions of sovereignty. One was the formulation of a rule that no case concerning the possession of land could begin without a writ from the king's court.[29] The other was the imposition of direct

[29] Glanvill, *De Legibus*, ch. 25, ". . . nemo tenetur respondere in curia domini suo sine praecepto domini regis vel eius capitalis iustitiae." See the comment on this rule in Woodbine's edition, p. 273.

taxes on the entire realm.[30] The rule requiring a royal
writ probably grew out of the doctrine that all lands
and rights possessed by free men in England were held
directly or indirectly of the King, and that therefore
he had responsibility for protecting lawful possession.
The right to tax grew out of the right of a lord to ask
financial aid from his vassals in an emergency. There
were plenty of emergencies at the end of the twelfth
century—the Third Crusade, the ransom of King
Richard from his German captivity, the long war with
Philip Augustus of France—and the aid paid by vassals could not possibly produce enough money to meet
the king's needs. It had to be expanded into a general
tax. Thus, both assertions of royal authority could be
justified as logical extensions of doctrines implicit in
feudal relationships, and certainly no one was yet
thinking in terms of sovereignty. But when feudal
theory had been elaborated to a point where it allowed
the king to regulate all justice and to tax all men,
suzerainty was coming very close to sovereignty. The
king surely had final authority in all legal matters; as
Glanvill says, decisions taken by the king and his
council were as binding as the *leges* of the Roman
emperors.[31] The king was also the final authority in
financial matters. He could not levy taxes at his own
pleasure, though it was hard to give a complete refusal
when the king asked for financial aid. But when it

[30] S. K. Mitchell, *Taxation in Medieval England* (New Haven,
1951), pp. 156-195.
[31] Glanvill, *De Legibus*, Prologue (p. 24 of the Woodbine
edition): "Leges namque Anglicanas licet non scriptas leges
appellari non videatur absurdum . . . eas scilicet quas super
dubiis in concilio definiendis, procerum quidem consilio et prin-
cipis accedente auctoritate constat esse promulgatas."

43

was agreed that a tax was needed, the king determined the nature of the tax, the procedure for collection and the exemptions to be allowed.[32] Perhaps more important, no one else in the realm could impose anything like a tax without royal permission. A baron who wanted to take scutage from his men or a town which wanted to repair its walls needed a royal writ before they could proceed.[33]

These precedents were used very effectively throughout the thirteenth century. Royal courts expanded their jurisdiction; taxes were imposed on the property of all men in the realm. By 1300 the king of England had not only many of the attributes of sovereignty, he had, and knew that he had, sovereign power. He made laws, formally and deliberately— laws which affected not only the procedure of the courts but the actual substance of rules about landholding—and these laws were binding on all men in the kingdom.[34] He taxed his lay subjects directly and repeatedly; he also asserted his right to tax the clergy without the assent of the pope.[35] He preferred, of course, to obtain the consent of his people to these measures, if only because consent made it easier to enforce his laws and to collect his taxes; but the devices used for obtaining consent show that England

[32] Examples in Stubbs, *Select Charters*, pp. 277, 348, 351, 356, 358.

[33] For scutage see Pollock and Maitland, *History of English Law*, I, 274, and T. Madox, *History of the Exchequer* (London, 1711), pp. 469-474. For the taxing power of towns, Pollock and Maitland, I, 662-663.

[34] *Statutes of the Realm*, I, 71, 106. For Edward's legislation see T.F.T. Plucknett, *Legislation of Edward I* (Oxford, 1949), pp. 2-10.

[35] W. Stubbs, *Constitutional History of England* (Oxford, 1906), II, 135-136, 140, 144-145, 147.

was a unified state with a recognized sovereign and final authority. The king might ask for advice or consent by consulting his court, his council, or his barons. Increasingly after 1260, he held his consultations in Parliament, an assembly of the magnates, knights elected by the shires, and representatives of the boroughs. But it was the king's will which gave authority to the decision reached in court, council, or the expanded council and High Court which was Parliament. It was only because England was a state with a strong sense of its identity that a few hundred men in Parliament could presume to give assent for the whole community. And it was only because the king had sovereign power that the assent of Parliament had any meaning. As Bracton had said two generations earlier, the king had all rights which pertained to secular power and to the government of the realm.[36]

Finally, and most significantly, during the thirteenth century it became clear that the basic loyalty of the English people (or at least of the people who were politically active) had shifted from family, community, and Church to the state.[37] Not that the old loyalties had vanished: men still worked to build up family wealth and power; they sought to gain or retain personal or communal privileges; they obeyed, in many matters, the behests of the clergy and the decisions of ecclesiastical courts. But all these lesser loyalties existed within the framework of the English

[36] Post, *Studies*, p. 342: the king has "omnia iura . . . quae ad coronam et laicalem pertinent potestatem et materialem gladium qui pertinet ad regni gubernaculum." See Helen Cam, "The Mediaeval English Franchise," *Speculum*, xxxii (1957), p. 440.

[37] J. R. Strayer, "Laicization of French and English Society in the Thirteenth Century," *Speculum*, xv (1940), 76-86.

state and were subordinated to the continuing existence and welfare of the English state. Thus when the barons rebelled, as they did in 1215 or 1258, or came near to rebellion, as they did in 1297, they had no thought of destroying the unity of England or the continuity of English institutions. When they believed that the policies of the central government were unwise or unjust, their remedy was to gain enough power so that they could use the central government to redress their grievances.[38] They expected the royal courts, properly instructed, to protect their rights; they expected the royal council, properly afforced with barons, to reverse unwise policies. They were not disappointed; they gained much of what they wanted by using existing institutions, and the existing institutions worked about as well under baronial control as they did under royal control.

To emphasize this point, the one privileged group which did not stay within the framework of the English state—the clergy—had less success with its protests. The clergy, in effect, had to recognize two sovereigns: the ecclesiastical sovereign who was the pope and the temporal sovereign who was the king. When the two sovereigns agreed, the clergy were helpless. They were not wholly within the structure of English government and could not use purely English institutions to protect themselves against the institutions of the universal Church. King and pope could make agreements to share taxes on the clergy which the clergy could not resist. When the two sovereigns disagreed, as they did in 1297 when Edward I wanted to

[38] The best statement of this position is R. F. Treharne, *The Baronial Plan of Reform* (Manchester, 1932).

tax the clergy without papal consent, the clergy were equally helpless. The Church could not protect them against the temporal power of the king. Their property was seized; the protection of the royal courts was explicitly withdrawn from them, and the king collected most of what he had asked. The clergy received almost no support from other classes, and many of the clergy themselves seem to have felt unhappy about the refusal to grant a tax.[39] The principle that the king's right to take money for defense of the realm had priority over all other obligations was fully established and was eventually accepted by the pope.[40] This priority of obligation could not have been recognized if there had not first been a shift in the scale of loyalties. The highest duty of every subject was now supposed to be the preservation and well-being of the state.

England went through these first stages of state-building with remarkable rapidity. This speed, in turn, made possible an unusual degree of uniformity in the English institutional structure. Local privileges and customs did not have time to harden into divisive institutions. The judicial and financial systems created in the eleventh and twelfth centuries could operate uniformly throughout the country. The absence of strongly entrenched provincial institutions improved the efficiency of the English government and reduced the need for a large number of professional administrators. There was no requirement for a hierarchy of

[39] See note 35, and F. M. Powicke, *The Thirteenth Century* (Oxford, 1953), pp. 674-678.

[40] *Registres de Boniface VIII*, no. 2354, the bull *Etsi de statu* allowed taxation of the clergy whenever it was needed for defense.

courts with an elaborate system of appeals from district to provincial to central authorities. The king's justices, sedentary or on circuit, could give final judgment at once and anywhere. There was no need for elaborate individual negotiations with hundreds of lords and communities when a tax was to be raised; the Council, and later the Parliament, could speak for the whole realm. Thus England did not have to have a large bureaucracy to control semi-autonomous provinces and to act as a liaison between provincial and central authorities. For example, at any one moment in the thirteenth century there were seldom more than twenty to twenty-five royal judges in England.[41] A single French province would require many more men.[42] Conversely, the English government could rely on unpaid local notables (knights and squires, mayors and aldermen) to do a great deal of the work of local administration. Energies which elsewhere were wasted in the defense of local privileges could be used in England to help the central government carry out its policies. This reliance on local notables was evident in the earliest stages of English state-building, and it remained typical of England down to the nineteenth century.

The very uniqueness of the English experience, however, made England a bad model for state-building. Few other countries moved as fast as England or were as free from internal divisions. As has already

[41] F. Palgrave, *Parliamentary Writs* (London, 1827), I, 382: in 1278 there were three justices of the King's Bench, five of the Court of Common Pleas, and twelve circuit judges.
[42] See my forthcoming study of *Les gens de justice du Languedoc*. By the end of the 13th century there were about forty royal judges in Languedoc alone.

been said, England was more like a large French province than it was like a continental kingdom. France, which had many provinces with widely differing institutions, was far more typical of the European political situation. And the fact that the French were the first to solve the nearly universal problem of creating a state out of virtually independent provinces made the French model preeminent in Europe. Most European states of the late medieval and early modern periods conformed, more or less closely, to the French pattern.

For France as for England, the two essential areas of development were justice and finance. But the French kings had to build slowly, and their early institutions were far simpler and less formalized than those of England. For example, while there was some sort of central audit of accounts in the late twelfth century, there was nothing like the specialized procedures of the English Exchequer. While the French royal court was more active and had greater prestige in 1200 than in 1100, it had neither the wide jurisdiction nor the established forms of law of the royal courts of England. The French chancery was neither as active in dealing with local authorities nor as exact in its language and procedure as its English counterpart. Down to 1200 royal institutions in France were fully effective only in the royal domain of the Ile de France, the area in which the king had direct lordship over most of the land. The king drew almost no revenue from outside his domain, and his court was only occasionally used by suitors who lived outside the Ile de France. Throughout most of the country the final authority was not the king but the duke, count, or lord who dominated a feudal principality.

Nevertheless, the building of institutions which were effective mainly in the royal domain increased the king's revenue, power, and prestige. By 1200 he was strong enough to attack and defeat the strongest provincial ruler, the king of England, who held most of the west of France. The northwestern provinces of Normandy, Anjou, and Poitou were taken over by the French king, and this started a process of annexation which continued throughout the century. By war, marriage, and inheritance, almost all the larger principalities were added to the royal domain; only Brittany, Guienne, Burgundy, and Flanders escaped.

This series of annexations posed serious questions for the French government. The relatively simple institutions which had been adequate to run a small royal domain would clearly have to be expanded and refined to deal with the greatly increased area and population now subject to the king. The new provinces had their own institutions and customs which were often more sophisticated and more specialized than those of the royal government. It was dangerous to try to change or suppress these provincial institutions, but how could a central government operate when each local administration followed different rules? The custom of Paris differed widely from the custom of Normandy, and the discrepancies were even greater between the northern customs and the law of the South which was strongly influenced by the learning of the Roman lawyers.

The basic solution for these problems was discovered by Philip Augustus (1180-1223), the king who was the real founder of the French state. He allowed each province to keep its own customs and institutions but sent out men from Paris to fill all important provincial offices. Thus Norman courts continued to enforce Norman law, but the presiding officers in these courts were not Normans but royal agents drawn largely from the old royal domain.[43] Provincial pride was placated, while the king kept effective control of his new possessions.

The formula was ingenious and made it possible to bind new provinces firmly to the kingdom, no matter how peculiar or deep-rooted their institutions were. The technique was useful as late as the seventeenth century, when France acquired Alsace. (By way of contrast, the English state, with its insistence on uniform institutions and laws, had great trouble in assimilating regions which had separate political traditions, such as the principalities of Wales or the petty kingdoms of Ireland.) But the emerging French state had to pay a heavy price for its flexibility. Local leaders were primarily concerned with the preservation of local customs and privileges; they distrusted the central government just as the central government distrusted them. They could not be used, to any great extent, in the work of local administration. In fact the basic rule of French administration was that no one should hold office in his native province.[44] The king

[43] J. R. Strayer, *The Administration of Normandy under St. Louis* (Cambridge, Mass., 1932), pp. 91-99; "Normandy and Languedoc," *Speculum*, xliv (1969), 1-12.

[44] *Ord.*, i, 67-75; neither a bailiff nor a seneschal should acquire property for himself or his family in the region he ruled (1254, often repeated). *Archives de la Ville de Montpellier*, ed. F. Castets and J. Berthelé (1895), i, 51; in 1317 Philip V dismissed the chief justice of the *sénéchaussée* of Beau-

51

had to create a bureaucracy to take care of provincial administration, a bureaucracy which grew at a rapid rate during the period of the formation of the French state. Moreover, while the French government was willing to tolerate a wide degree of diversity in local practices, there had to be some uniformity in such matters as taxation, some way of reconciling conflicting local interests, some means of asserting the ultimate authority of the king. Thus France had to develop a many-layered administrative structure. Local officials were supervised by provincial officials who were supervised by regional officials who were supervised by councils, courts, and chambers sitting in Paris. There was a constant flow of orders, rebukes, judicial decisions, and requests for information running from central to local authorities, and an equally constant flow of protests, appeals, excuses, and explanations running the other way. The complexity of the French administrative system was especially harmful in a period of slow communications; it meant that the central government could never make effective use of its human and material resources. England, with less than one-fifth the population and probably much less than one-fourth the wealth of France, was often able to match France man for man and pound for pound in periods of conflict.

---

caire-Nîmes because he was a native, and royal ordinances forbade anyone to be a judge in the district in which he was born. In England, on the contrary, a sheriff had to hold land in the county he governed; see *Rot. Parl.*, I, 282, 353, 465; *Statutes of the Realm*, I, 160, 174; *Cal. Fine Rolls*, IV, 463, 467-468: a thoroughly experienced sheriff who had served in Wiltshire 1330-1332, and in Dorsetshire 1333-1335 was not allowed to become a sheriff of Devonshire in 1335 because he held no land there.

This is not to say that the French system was a failure. It was the only one which could have worked under existing conditions. France was a mosaic state, made up of many pieces, and the bureaucracy was the cement which held all the pieces together. If the cement sometimes got so thick that it obscured the pattern of government, this was better than letting it get so thin that the state fell apart. French methods did make it possible to create a state out of provinces and regions with widely divergent characteristics. And because most of the European states which eventually emerged were mosaic states like France, they tended to follow the French model.

During the thirteenth century the sovereignty of the French king was clearly established. Externally, almost everyone, including the pope, recognized that he had no temporal superior.[45] Internally, the king insisted that he was the final judge in all cases, that, no matter how great the rights or how extensive the privileges of a province or a lord, appeals eventually ran to the king's court in Paris. In fact this right of final judgment was the one right which was constantly asserted in areas where the king otherwise had little power, such as the duchy of Aquitaine or the county of Flanders.[46] Fully as extensive in theory, though

[45] *Decr. Greg.*, IX, 4, 17, 13; in 1202 Innocent III said that the king of France "superiorem in temporalibus minime recognoscit"; this became official Church doctrine. A little later someone coined the phrase that "rex (the king of France) est imperator in regno suo," i.e., he has supreme temporal power. This interpretation has been challenged by F. Calasso, *I Glossatori e la teoria della sovranità* (Milan, 1951), but see Sergio Mochi Onory, *Fonti Canonistiche dell'idea moderna dello stato* (Milan, 1951), and Post, *Studies*, pp. 453-480.

[46] *Olim*, II, 142, 244, 300 (Flanders), I, 284, II, 94, 97, 138, 148, 236 (Aquitaine). *Olim*, II, 3-8: a citation of Edward I to

less extensive in practice, was the king's right to make ordinances for the general welfare.[47] Royal ordinances might not be enforced with great zeal in all parts of the realm, but it was difficult to deny their validity. In the same way, the right of the king to impose taxes, especially taxes for the defense of the kingdom, was generally recognized.[48] In practice, there might be some haggling over rates, some sharing of proceeds with the more powerful lords, but it was almost impossible to deny completely a royal demand for money.

There was also, as there was in England, a clear shift of loyalty to the state. As in England, there was no popular support for the pope when he tried to forbid taxation of the clergy. In fact there was strong resentment against the clergy for not sharing in the

Parlement was the excuse for the occupation of Gascony in 1294; *ibid.* 394-396: Parlement, by intervening in the affairs of Flemish towns in 1295, weakened the court and prepared the way for the later occupation of Flanders.

[47] The key passage is Beaumanoir, *Coutumes de Beauvaisis*, paras. 1512-1515: the king can make "establissemens" for the common good; all must obey them; the king can punish anyone who breaks them; but new "establissemens" must be made for reasonable cause and "par grant conseil." There was less significant legislation in France than in England down to 1300, but the authority of a royal ordinance was fully as great as that of an English statute, e.g., embargoes on the export of horses and arms were enforced even in distant provinces, *Ord.*, xi, 353; Champollion-Figeac, *Lettres de rois* (Paris, 1839), i, 285, 298.

[48] In general, see my article on "Consent to Taxation under Philip the Fair" in J. R. Strayer and C. H. Taylor, *Studies in Early French Taxation* (Cambridge, Mass., 1939). Specifically, *Hist. Litt.*, xxxvi, 515; Pierre Jame, a lawyer of Montpellier who had no great love for Philip the Fair, admitted that the king could levy taxes without consent for the defense of the realm. This merely repeated the admissions of Boniface VIII in 1297 (*Reg. Bonif. VIII* no. 2354) that the king could tax even the clergy for defense of the realm.

defense of the realm—resentment which was so bitter that it worried the bishops.[49] Once the tax question was settled to the satisfaction of the king, a new controversy arose over the right of secular authorities to arrest and try a bishop accused of treason. In the propaganda war which followed, the pope had clearly the worst of it. His denunciations of the king produced no visible effect on any segment of the French population. The king's agents, on the other hand, gained the support of all the politically significant groups in France even when they made fantastic charges against the orthodoxy and morality of the pope. The nobility, the towns, and almost all the clergy assented to a plan to call a Church Council to judge the pope.[50] The consent of the nobles and of the townsmen probably expressed their true feelings; they honestly believed that the pope was trying to destroy France, and they felt that they must defend the kingdom even against the heir of St. Peter. The clergy were undoubtedly under pressure to conform and must have been dubious about the validity of the charges against the pope. But if the clergy were not enthusiastic supporters of the king, they showed no great zeal for the papal cause. They produced no martyrs; they did not even criticize royal policy. Apparently they felt that it was better to preserve harmony and unity in France than to defend the reputation of the pope. In the final crisis, when the king sent an armed band to arrest the pope, and when the pope died as a re-

[49] P. Dupuy, *Histoire du differend* (Paris, 1655), *preuves*, p. 26.

[50] The essential documents are printed in G. Picot, *Documents relatifs aux États Généraux et Assemblées réunis sous Philippe le Bel* (Paris, 1901).

sult of shock and ill-treatment, there was no wave of indignation in France, even among the clergy. Succeeding popes found it impossible to stir up any interest in the case. In the end the king was completely exonerated, and his agents were given relatively light penances (which they never performed).[51] Just as a practical matter, it was evident that it was safer to be loyal to the king than to the pope.

The change, however, went beyond motives of personal security and advancement. Some men—mostly lawyers and royal officials—were beginning to idealize their state. There had long been a cult devoted to the king—the only European monarch who could claim that he was annointed with oil brought directly from Heaven, heir of Charlemagne, healer of the sick.[52] By 1300 there was a cult of the kingdom of France. France was a holy land, where piety, justice, and scholarship flourished. Like the Israelites of old the French were a chosen people, deserving and enjoying divine favor. To protect France was to serve God.[53] As these ideas spread—and soon after 1400 they were known by a peasant girl living on the extreme eastern frontier of the kingdom—loyalty to the state became more than a necessity or a convenience; it was now a virtue.

[51] R. Holtzmann, *Wilhelm von Nogaret* (Freiburg i. B., 1898), chs. 4, 7.
[52] Two excellent books on this theme are M. Bloch, *Les rois thaumaturges* (Paris, 1961), and P. E. Schramm, *Der König von Frankreich* (Weimar, 1939), chs. 5-8.
[53] J. R. Strayer, "France: The Holy Land, the Chosen People, and the Most Christian King," *Action and Conviction in Early Modern Europe*, ed. T. K. Rabb and J. E. Siegel (Princeton, 1969), pp. 3-16.

By 1300 it was evident that the dominant political form in Western Europe was going to be the sovereign state. The universal Empire had never been anything but a dream; the universal Church had to admit that defense of the individual state took precedence over the liberties of the Church or the claims of the Christian commonwealth. Loyalty to the state was stronger than any other loyalty, and for a few individuals (largely government officials) loyalty to the state was taking on some of the overtones of patriotism.[54]

Nevertheless, while the sovereign state of 1300 was stronger than any competing political form, it was still not very strong. Loyalty to the state might override all other loyalties, but in an age when other loyalties had been weakened, loyalty to the state could be dominant without being very intense. It took four to five centuries for European states to overcome their weaknesses, to remedy their administrative deficiencies, and to bring lukewarm loyalty up to the white heat of nationalism.

The first two centuries after 1300 were especially difficult. One might say that Europeans had created their state system only in the nick of time, for the fourteenth century saw a series of disasters which scarcely encouraged political innovation. A great economic depression, one of the longest in history, began

[54] Kantorowicz, *The King's Two Bodies*, pp. 232-262 (the section is entitled "Pro Patria Mori").

in the 1280's.[55] Western Europe had reached its limits in agricultural production, commercial exchanges, and industrial activity. Until new techniques, new markets, and new sources of supply were developed, stagnation was certain and regression likely. Population was pressing heavily on the land, and the famines and plagues which eventually reduced the pressure did not improve the morale of the survivors. The Black Death, which struck heavily about the middle of the century and which returned several times before 1400, very nearly wiped out some local governments and killed many potential leaders. Economic and physical insecurity was reflected in political instability. However we define them, there were certainly more riots, rebellions, and civil wars in the fourteenth century than in the thirteenth century.

Depression, famine, and plague could not have been warded off by any fourteenth-century government; the necessary knowledge and techniques simply did not exist. Governments might have avoided the long and costly wars which aggravated the suffering and the demoralization of the people. But in a sense the wars were necessary to complete the development of a system of sovereign states. Sovereignty requires independence from any outside power and final authority over men who live within certain boundaries. But in 1300 it was not clear who was independent and who was not, and it was difficult to draw definite bound-

[55] A good account of the depression is the chapter by L. Genicot in *The Cambridge Economic History of Europe*, ed. M. M. Postan, 2nd ed. (Cambridge, Eng., 1966), I, 660-741. I have argued that the depression began in the 1280's in "Economic Conditions in the County of Beaumont-le-Roger," *Speculum*, XXVI (1951), 277-287.

aries in a Europe which had known only overlapping spheres of influence and fluctuating frontier zones. The great kingdoms of the West might have solid cores, but on their fringes were areas which might or might not be incorporated in the state: Wales and Scotland in the case of England, Brittany, Guienne, Flanders, and the rubble of the old Middle Kingdom in the case of France. England conquered Wales but did not absorb Scotland; France conquered Guienne, annexed Brittany and many small territories along the eastern frontier, but failed to gain Flanders. It took generations of hard fighting to reach these results, but at least one can say that the results were positive; they helped to define the areas controlled by the two most advanced European states.

To a lesser degree, the same results were achieved in Germany and in Italy, though on a smaller and less permanent scale. In the absence of strong kingdoms, each German principality and each Italian city claimed the attributes of sovereignty. Petty wars, marriage alliances, and divisions among heirs meant that the size and number of states fluctuated wildly. But in spite of the confusion a certain number of reasonably stable states emerged: for example, a Tuscan state dominated by Florence and a southeast German state dominated by the Habsburgs.

On the other hand, many of the wars of the fourteenth and fifteenth centuries checked, or even set back the process of state-building. In an age when the economy was stagnant, if not regressive, the easiest way for a ruler to increase his income and power was to try to gain control of new territories, even if those territories lay within the boundaries of an already established state. The Hundred Years' War was especially vicious and prolonged because it was a war in which the efforts of the French monarchy to complete the work of consolidating and defining the boundaries of its territories were countered by efforts of English kings to increase their holdings of French lands. England was often allied with Brittany, Flanders, or Burgundy in this attempt to detach certain provinces from the control of the French monarchy, and on at least two occasions (the Treaty of Calais in 1360 and the Treaty of Troyes in 1420) it looked as if the attempt were going to succeed. It seems evident to us that the English kings never had the resources to hold and govern large parts of France, but this was not so evident to contemporaries. For a century and a half the French monarchy had to concentrate much of its energy in defending lands and rights that it had already acquired by 1300. For a century and a half the English monarchy devoted much of its energy to the task of splintering the kingdom of France. War sometimes stimulates the growth of administrative institutions, but this particular war was so exhausting for both sides that it discouraged the normal development of the apparatus of the state. There was a tendency to postpone structural reforms, to solve problems on an ad hoc basis rather than by the creation of new agencies of government, to sacrifice efficiency for immediate results. The same weaknesses appeared in Germany and in Spain. Only in Italy, where wars were fought on a smaller and less devastating scale, was there noticeable improvement in administrative techniques in the fourteenth and early fifteenth centuries.

To some extent, the success of thirteenth-century rulers in building states had made fourteenth-century wars necessary and possible. The same success had created another problem, that of gaining the support of the propertied and politically active classes. Medieval states, as we have seen, were law-states. They had acquired their power largely by developing their judicial institutions and by protecting the property rights of the possessing classes. The most typical expression of internal sovereignty was the right to give final judgment in a high court. A corollary of this emphasis on law was an emphasis on the right of consent. Existing usages, guaranteed by law, were a form of property. They could not be changed without due process, any more than property could be seized without due process. Thus consent was required for all acts of government, either explicit consent in the form of a grant by subjects or implicit consent to the acts of a court. This emphasis on consent was not just theory, though it received theoretical formulation in thirteenth-century political thinking.[56] It was an inescapable political fact. No state had the military power, the bureaucratic personnel, or even the information needed to impose unpopular measures on opposition groups that had any political and social standing. The cooperation of local leaders

[56] Post, *Studies*, pp. 91-238. A nice example of the seriousness with which the theory was taken may be found in E. Martène and U. Durand, *Thesaurus Novus* (Paris, 1717), II, col. 508. Charles I of Sicily imposed a general subvention on his kingdom in 1267. Pope Clement IV immediately rebuked him, saying that the act had caused great scandal and that he should call a meeting of barons, prelates, and leading men of the towns to discuss when and how such a tax should be imposed.

was essential for implementing any administrative decision. In the fourteenth century it became difficult to get this cooperation.

There were several reasons for this difficulty. In the first place, the stagnant or declining economy placed the possessing classes under heavy financial pressure. They tried to avoid or lessen the burden of taxation; they also tried to secure appointments or commissions from the government that increased their income without adding greatly to their responsibilities. Local magnates, for example, were often asked to assure local defense and were given large sums of money to hire soldiers and improve fortifications. Much of this money was wasted or diverted to other purposes. The local military forces that were raised were often used by local leaders to enforce doubtful claims to the property of weaker neighbors, or at times for pure acts of banditry. At a higher level, the great lords intrigued for positions in the central government. The losers in the competition became disloyal; the winners used their jobs to enrich themselves and their followers. And at times the jealousies between baronial factions became so acute that they led to civil war.

This resurgence of baronial power has sometimes been described as "bastard feudalism." It certainly caused some breakdown in control of local government, but it did not create a really feudal situation. No enduring principalities were created; power and wealth shifted rapidly from one factional leader to another. In fact, with one or two exceptions, the purpose of the political game was not to create a new government, but rather to get control of some part of the existing government and use that control for selfish purposes. The retainers of baronial leaders were not rewarded by grants of fiefs; they were paid from such revenues of the central government as the baronial leaders controlled. Therefore, while the intrigues and quarrels of the nobles and their followers weakened local and central governments, they were never pursued so far as to destroy existing institutions. The basic structure of government had to be preserved in order to generate the revenues sought by the upper classes.

It is also true that the propertied classes could often thwart the wishes of the government without resorting to intrigues or violence. The state itself provided the machinery for obstruction. In the twelfth and thirteenth centuries the chief aim of both rulers and responsible members of society was to build up the competence and the prestige of courts of law so that most disputes could be settled by peaceful means. It had taken a great deal of persistent pressure to persuade the propertied classes to accept the jurisdiction of the courts, and no government wanted to risk weakening established legal procedures. But barons, prelates, and the self-governing towns soon found that if they agreed to play the game according to the new rules, they could often thwart the government more effectively by legal obstructionism than by armed resistance. Given the difficulties of travel and communication, courts had to act very slowly if they were to act justly. It might take years to decide whether a claim for local privilege was justified, and, when the decision was finally made, the same claim might be raised again in slightly different form. In countries which had an elaborate system of appellate jurisdiction (such as France) delays were particularly great,[57] but justice was by no means swift even in England, which had a rather simple court structure. Governments did not have the time or the administrative personnel to deal with all the protests which were made. It was easier to compromise, to make some reductions in financial demands or some grants of exemptions and privileges.[58] The only alternative was to turn over local administration and local justice to local leaders, such as the English Justices of the Peace. Such an arrangement prevented some (not all) of the protests, but it meant that government policy was interpreted, and often modified, by men whom the government did not control.

A special example of the use of official machinery to limit the freedom of action of the government can be seen in the development of representative assemblies. The idea of political representation is one of the great discoveries of medieval governments; the Greeks and the Romans may have made a few tentative moves in this direction, but they had never explored

[57] An early example was the suit in which the king claimed, as against the bishop of Mende, jurisdiction over the Gévaudan: R. Michel, *L'administration royale dans la sénéchaussée de Beaucaire* (Paris, 1910), p. 454; the suit began in 1269: J. Roucaute and M. Saché, *Lettres de Philippe le Bel relatives au pays de Gévaudan* (Mende, 1897), pp. vii-xii, 174-195; it was settled by a compromise in 1307, but (pp. 67-69, 202-208) the nobles of the region appealed, and their appeal was not squashed until 1341. For a discussion of delays in legal procedure in a later period see B. Guenée, *Tribunaux et gens de justice dans le bailliage de Senlis (1380-1550)* (Paris, 1963), pp. 221-250.

[58] M. Rey, *Le domaine du roi et les finances extraordinaires sous Charles VI* (Paris, 1965), pp. 181-182, 269-275 lists some of the exemptions from taxation that existed in France in the late 14th century.

the technique thoroughly. In medieval Europe, on the other hand, representative assemblies appeared everywhere: in Italy, Spain, and southern France early in the thirteenth century; in England, northern France, and Germany anywhere from fifty to one hundred years later. There has been considerable argument about the origins of these assemblies, but most scholars would agree that they were closely associated with the growth of medieval courts and medieval jurisprudence.[59] The principles that important decisions should be made publicly, that customs should not be changed without general agreement, that consent was necessary when the superior needed extraordinary additions to his income, that "what touches all should be approved by all," could be

[59] The literature on this subject is enormous, and only a few books can be cited. C. H. McIlwain led the way with *The High Court of Parliament* (New Haven, 1910). D. Pasquet, *An Essay on the Origins of the House of Commons* (Cambridge, Eng., 1925), stresses political aspects of early Parliaments, while H. G. Richardson and G. O. Sayles have emphasized the judicial side of Parliament in their articles in the *Transactions of the Royal Historical Society*, xi (1929) and in the *Bulletin of the Institute for Historical Research*, v (1927-1928) and vi (1928-1929). See also their *Parliaments and Great Councils* (London, 1961). For France the old book of H. Hervieu, *Recherches sur les premiers États Généraux*, is completely out-of-date, and C. Soule's recent work, *Les États Généraux de France* (Heule, 1968), is too juridical and has little to say about the early period. There are some very helpful remarks in the articles of C. H. Taylor on early French assemblies published in *Speculum*, xi (1936), xiii (1938), xiv (1939), xxix (1954), xliii (1968). T. N. Bisson, *Assemblies and Representation in Languedoc in the Thirteenth Century* (Princeton, 1964), is an excellent treatment of early assemblies in southern France. For Spain see Post, *Studies*, pp. 70-79; for Italy, A. Marongiu, *L'Istituto parlamentare in Italia dalle origini al 1500* (Milan, 1956), and Post, *Studies*, pp. 80-90. Marongiu's book has been adapted and translated by S. J. Woolf as *Medieval Parliaments* (London, 1966).

found in treatises on feudal law, customary law, and the revived Roman law.[60] Even more important, these ideas formed part of the general climate of opinion; they were held by men who had never read a book or heard a lecture on law.

Thus all governments had to find a way by which the politically active, propertied classes could give consent. It was already common practice for a few men to speak for a large corporate group, such as town or monastery, in a court of law; it seemed reasonable to allow a few men to represent their groups when customs were being altered or when taxes were being imposed. These representatives could be brought to enlarged meetings of high courts in order to hear the reasons for decisions; they could be called to special meetings, national or regional, to hear matters of general concern discussed. Consent was expressed more by the act of appearing at the court or at the meeting than by formal voting; it is several generations before we hear of debates and votes.

The assemblies satisfied the feeling of subjects that they should be consulted; they also made it easier for rulers to achieve their objectives. At the least, an assembly gave the government a chance to explain its point of view to influential men; at the best, an assembly could give consent that bound all the propertied classes. In fact, rulers at first seem to have been rather more enthusiastic about representative assemblies than were their subjects. An assembly almost

[60] The most thorough studies of these topics may be found in Post, *Studies*, chs. 3 and 4. Post takes a very strong position on the influence of the two laws and the importance of legal forms, but he cites the critics who would modify his position.

always gave the ruler political or financial support; for the subjects called to the meeting it meant a loss of time and, very often, the imposition of new financial burdens.

A representative assembly was a tool of government, just as a court was. And just as subjects learned how to use courts to obstruct government actions, so they learned how to use assemblies. These meetings, where important men of all classes came together, were convenient occasions for voicing grievances, for demanding investigations and reforms. Assemblies had little follow-up power, but they could make officials unhappy for a few weeks, and sometimes for as much as a year when they persuaded the ruler to establish an auditing or reforming commission.[61] More important, assemblies almost never granted as much money as a ruler requested. A flat denial was rare—the ruler, after all, probably had some reason for his request—but complete acceptance of government plans was rare too. Usually the form or the rate

[61] E. B. Fryde, "Parliament and the French War, 1336-1340," *Essays in Medieval History Presented to Bertie Wilkinson,* eds. T. A. Sandquist and M. R. Powicke (Toronto, 1969), pp. 250-269, shows how unhappy the English Parliament could make the government during a crucial period. R. Cazelles, *La société politique et la crise de la royauté sous Philippe de Valois* (Paris, 1958), pp. 224-225, 427-428; the Estates of 1347 forced some temporary reforms on the government. J. B. Henneman, "The Black Death and Royal Taxation in France, 1347-1351," *Speculum,* xliii (1968), 407-412, has shown how regional assemblies gained the right to appoint their own collectors and auditors of taxes in 1348. *Ord.,* iii, 19; this practice was extended to the whole kingdom in 1355 and continued for some years until the king gained control of the collectors. In England there are several examples of special commissions appointed by request of Parliament to make sure that taxes were spent only for approved purposes, e.g., *Rot. Parl.,* iii, 7 (1377), 35-36 (1378), 523ff (1404).

of taxation was altered so that it would bear less heavily on the taxpayers, and especially on those of the privileged classes. Argument and political pressure might persuade the assembly to increase its grant, but seldom to a point where it was really adequate.

For a long time there was no easy way to deal with this kind of obstruction. There was a tendency to settle for lump sums or for conventional payments rather than to prolong fruitless discussions. Thus in France a regional assembly might promise that it would raise so many thousand pounds by its own devices in lieu of taxation.[62] In England the government in 1334 gave up trying to assess personal property and agreed that the conventional value of a 10 percent tax was 34,000 pounds.[63] As long as assemblies could hold down the yield of taxes (and in some regions they retained this power into the sixteenth century or even later) further development of European states was hampered. On the other hand, when assemblies lost this power (as they did in France), a certain amount of goodwill and cooperation was lost too. Government officials or tax-farmers might squeeze the peasants, but the privileged classes (including the bourgeoisie) managed by legal or illegal means to avoid a considerable part of their proper share of taxation. Unequal distribution of taxes certainly reduced

[62] J. B. Henneman, "Financing the Hundred Years' War," *Speculum*, xlii (1967), 280-292, gives some nice examples for 1340. For later years see his article cited in note 61, pp. 420-424.

[63] J. F. Willard, *Parliamentary Taxes on Personal Property* (Cambridge, Mass., 1934), pp. 11-13, 344-345. See his remarks on conventional valuation, pp. 138-144. The official rate was 10 percent on personal property in towns and 6 2/3 percent in the country.

the income of the state and probably slowed down economic recovery.

Finally, certain weaknesses that were inherent in the governmental structure as it had developed in the twelfth and thirteenth centuries became apparent in the fourteenth century. As we have seen, the first professional or semi-professional officials were those who collected and accounted for revenue from the domain. They had other duties: administration of justice, keeping of the peace, local defense; but these duties were considered part of the task of preserving and if possible increasing the income of the ruler. Thus the early bureaucracy in England and in France was one of estate-managers, and the estate-manager outlook continued to dominate the bureaucracy even after new and more specialized offices were developed. The estate-manager mentality was essential to the early stages of state-building. It was only when a ruler had regular and adequate revenues that he could hope to extend and intensify his authority over his vassals or turn vague rights of suzerainty into rights of sovereignty. But the estate-manager mentality had dangerous limitations. It was a mentality that loved routine and stability and resented uncertainty and unpredictable change. The ideal situation for the estate-manager was one in which a register could be prepared listing all sources of income, and in which the same income could be collected year after year. Once the great effort had been made to prepare a list or lists of sources of income there was a natural reluctance to repeat the effort. Old lists were used year after year, even though every year they became more out-of-date. Corrections, of course, were made, but the basic idea was that there was a fixed body of rights and revenues which would fluctuate only within manageable limits.

Such attitudes did little harm as long as rights and revenues came primarily from the domain. Land, a local court, a town marketplace: such things did not vanish even if officials were working with lists that were a century or more old. In a period in which prices were rising only slowly, a fixed income based on ancient valuations was no disaster; it was better than the decline in income which would have occurred if the estate-managers had not done their work conscientiously.

The situation became very different when rulers began to depend on taxation. Now what was needed was a new estimate (of hearths, land, income, and so forth) every time there was a new tax. Great variations in the tax base and in the yield were to be expected, especially if experiments were tried with different kinds of taxes. The old bureaucracy could not adjust to these new demands. Granted, there was serious understaffing; granted also (as we have seen), there was opposition by assemblies and tax evasion by the privileged classes. Nevertheless, after a promising start towards securing accurate and regularly revised assessments, a tendency to use conventional estimates and to accept conventional sums became dominant. This trend was especially strong in the large kingdoms. Small political units, such as the Italian city-states, came fairly close to getting accurate valuations of property, even in the most troubled periods of the fourteenth century.[64] But by the mid-

[64] The most thorough study of the finances of an Italian city-

70

dle of that century the number of hearths listed in France or the amount of personal property assessed for taxation in England bore no relationship to the real facts.[65]

Another problem of fourteenth-century bureaucracies was the tendency of each department to turn itself into a semi-autonomous, self-perpetuating corporation, not unlike a guild. Procedures became formal and rather inflexible; recruitment was largely limited to relatives, clerks, and protégés of men already in office; most senior officials served long periods of apprenticeship in minor posts where they became imbued with the traditions of their department. Of course, autonomy was never complete, and routine was never unbreakable. The ruler and his chief councillors could appoint men to high office who had had little or no connection with the agency they were to direct. Even if the head of a great department had risen from the ranks, he was the personal choice of the ruler and was naturally amenable to the wishes of the ruler. In times of emergency the ruler could speed up or bypass formal procedures. But personal intervention by the king and his advisers seldom went very deep into the bureaucratic structure and seldom persisted long enough to cause substantial changes. Middle-

state is the forthcoming book of W. Bowsky on the Commune of Siena. Some of his conclusions are summarized in his article, "The Impact of the Black Death upon Sienese Government and Society," *Speculum*, xxxix (1964), 11-13, 21-23.

[65] Borrelli de Serres, *Recherches sur divers services publics* (Paris, 1909), iii, section 5 and esp. pp. 406-433. A. Higounet-Nadal, *Les Comptes de la taille de Perigueux* (Paris, 1965), pp. 66-71, finds that in the 1360's the *feu fiscal* was still close to the *feu réel*, but that this equivalence soon vanished. For English assessments see note 63.

level officials clung to their old traditions or reverted to them as soon as pressure from the top was relaxed. The vast mass of ordinary financial and judicial business had to be conducted according to fixed department procedures if it was to be conducted at all. The existence of bureaucratic inertia is, of course, not surprising; it can be found in many other times and places. What is surprising is its strength in the fourteenth and fifteenth centuries, and the success of established departments in protecting obsolete and inefficient procedures.

This is not to say that there were no reforms and no innovations. There were men who were conscious of weaknesses in their departments, men like Bishop Stapledon who greatly improved the organization of the English Exchequer in the 1320's.[66] There were attempts to define and refine procedures, as in the fourteenth-century ordinances on the *Parlement* of Paris.[67] In France there was a tendency to create new departments of government, and also to create provincial replicas of old departments. Thus at the end of the fourteenth century a *Chambre* (or *Cour*) *des Aides* was established to deal with income from taxation while the older *Chambre des Comptes* handled revenue from the domain.[68] In the fifteenth century a separate *Parlement* (or high court) and a *Chambre des Comptes* were created for Langue-

[66] T. F. Tout, *Chapters in the Administrative History of Mediaeval England* (Manchester, 1937), II, 211-221, 258-267.

[67] *Ord.*, I, 647, 702, 718; II, 219-224; III, 653; IV, 512; VII, 224; XIII, 479; and many others.

[68] G. Dupont-Ferrier, *Les origines et le premier siècle de la chambre ou cour des aides* (Paris, 1933); M. Rey, *Les finances royales sous Charles VI* (Paris, 1965), pp. 543-559.

72

doc[69] (and eventually for other regions as well). Such measures doubtless saved some time in travel, eased congestion at the center, and flattered provincial pride. They did not, however, change the mentality of the bureaucracy. Judges in the new *Parlements* quickly adopted the traditions and the corporate spirit of the original *Parlement* of Paris. The new financial agencies were no more successful than the old in obtaining accurate assessments of property and income, or in getting into the treasury anything like an adequate percentage of the sums that were due. In fact, the French had increased the size of their bureaucracy enough to make the government more complicated but not enough to make it capable of dealing directly with the people. Many taxes were collected by tax-farmers and, in the case of the *gabelle* (salt tax), by merchants; such men oppressed the people without increasing the king's revenues.[70]

England followed a rather different path. Few new departments were created and there was less expansion of the bureaucracy. The expansion came rather in the amount of service required from unpaid local notables, especially through the establishment of the office of Justice of the Peace. By the end of the fourteenth century these justices, country gentry and urban oligarchs, were responsible for the enforcement of statutes and administrative orders at the local level, for the arrest of lawbreakers, and for the trial of minor offenses. Local notables also retained responsibility for the collection of taxes. Thus the

---

[69] H. Gilles, *Les États de Languedoc au XVe siècle* (Toulouse, 1965), pp. 250-263.

[70] M. Rey, *Le domaine du roi*, pp. 178-179, 233-244 (farm of sales taxes), 184-185 (salt), 195-198.

English bureaucracy could remain relatively small and uncomplicated. It was not very efficient, but it was inefficient at less cost than that of most other states. And when the king and the propertied classes were able to agree on their objectives, the English system, thanks to the support of local notables, might be more efficient than that of other countries in mobilizing human and financial resources.

The basic problems of late medieval government, however, were solved neither by the French practice of increasing the size and complexity of the bureaucracy nor by the English practice of demanding more work from unpaid local notables. These basic problems can be grouped under two main heads: first, the inevitable gap between policymakers and bureaucrats became dangerously wide; second, partly because of this gap and partly for other reasons, neither policymakers nor bureaucrats showed much skill in devising techniques for dealing with the recurring crises of the fourteenth and fifteenth centuries.

The gap between policymakers and bureaucrats had not been serious down to 1300, but in the fourteenth century it was widened by faults of both groups. Policy was made by the king and his Council, a body composed of members of the royal family, royal favorites, heads of baronial factions, and the chief officers of household and government departments. Attendance of princes and nobles was sporadic; often the Council was composed completely of household and administrative officials. Such a Council could deal with routine matters of internal administration and could implement policies already agreed on, for example, the mustering or supply of an army. But when the great (and expensive) questions of peace and war, truces and alliances came up, the princes and baronial leaders had to be consulted. Such men were usually not very well informed, nor did they work very hard to repair the gaps in their information. But even if they had been eager to remedy their ignorance, they would have found it difficult to do so. As we have seen, professional bureaucrats with their increasingly rigid routines could not have supplied up-to-date information about internal affairs. No one was charged with collecting information about foreign countries, certainly not the professional bureaucrats, certainly not the aristocratic members of the Council. Thus major policy decisions were made on the basis of very limited knowledge and were often influenced by the personal ambitions or grievances of the great men. A campaign might be planned simply to give a member of the royal family a chance to distinguish himself by leading an army and enrich himself by collecting booty and ransoms. A tax raised to support a campaign might be dissipated in gifts, pensions, and inflated payments for inadequate amounts of military service. This kind of irresponsibility on the part of the policymakers reached its height when the king was weak or incapable, for example, in the reigns of Charles VI of France or Henry VI of England. But even strong and able kings who had chosen the best councillors they could find had trouble developing reasonable and continuing lines of policy. They tended to overestimate their financial and military resources and underestimate the need for internal reforms.

As was suggested above, the professional bureaucracy had little chance to influence policy decisions, partly because it lacked the information necessary to sway the opinions of the great men, partly because it had insulated itself from politics by creating strong corporative traditions and structures. Even the heads of departments who sat on the Council were more apt to be consulted about ways and means than about the substance of policy. It is true that careful attention to ways and means might have changed the structure and improved the revenues of governments and thus have led to changes in policy. But the most carefully drafted plans for administrative reform, such as the Walton Ordinances of 1338[71] in England or the ordinances of the Marmousets in France in 1389,[72] were never fully implemented. The princes and great nobles distrusted reforms that might have lessened their power and income; the financial pressures of war discouraged efforts to reduce dishonesty and inefficiency. Fifty thousand pounds in a period of crisis were worth more than one hundred thousand pounds produced two years too late by reform measures. In short the policymakers put additional strains on an ill-informed and badly organized bureaucracy by erratic and shortsighted decisions. The bureaucracy had to jump from expedient to expedient to meet sudden demands for money and action; it seldom had time to make long-range plans.

Admitting all this, there was in the later Middle Ages a curious lack of imagination on the part of both the amateur and professional members of the govern-

[71] Tout, *Chapters*, III, 69-79.
[72] Rey, *Le domaine du roi*, pp. 71-72, 100, 103-104, 135-136, 175-176, 282-283. The life of one of the leaders of this reform movement was written by H. Moranvillé, *Étude sur la vie de Jean le Mercier* (Paris, 1888), in *Mémoires présentés par divers savants à l'Académie des inscriptions et belles-lettres*, 2e s., t.6.

ments of the larger European states. In the first period of state-building—roughly from the eleventh through the thirteenth centuries—rulers and their advisers had shown great ingenuity in creating new institutions and techniques of government. The men who staffed the new institutions—one can scarcely call them professionals until the thirteenth century—had shown equal ingenuity in expanding the activity and perfecting the procedures of the office in which they served. But in the fourteenth century (with the exception of some of the Italian city-states), governments seemed less willing than before to assume new responsibilities or to develop new organs of administration. The only fully organized, permanently constituted agencies were the chanceries, the courts, and the office or offices that dealt with the ruler's income and expenditures. The only professional civil servants were those concerned with financial matters, with the administration of justice, and with the keeping of records. Some, but by no means all, of the men in charge of local administration could be added to this group, though it is often difficult to draw the line between the experienced amateur, whose chief ties remained with his district or town, and the budding professional, who hoped to gain eventually a position in the central government. But, however we describe the departments of government or define professional civil servants, it is evident that many functions of a modern state were either not being performed at all, or were being performed badly. One would scarcely expect a medieval government to concern itself with problems of health or education. But one would expect, in an age of economic instability, internal insecurity, and almost constant warfare, that specialized agencies would have emerged to regulate the economy, to suppress crime and disorder, to organize the armed forces, and to conduct interstate relations. Except in Italy, such agencies did not emerge, and even in Italy they were rudimentary.

Lack of money and a strong tradition of local self-regulation explain some of these deficiencies. It was to be a long time before any large state could afford an adequate police force. Meanwhile the towns had their watchmen and the county or provincial administrators had their "sergeants" (to use the French phrase)—a handful of men who could be used for anything from process-serving to small military operations.

Internal economic activities were controlled almost entirely by local authorities—by the landowners in the country districts, by town governments or organizations of master workmen in urban areas. There were some clumsy attempts to regulate foreign trade for political or economic advantages. The most common practice was to forbid export of precious metals, or food, or horses and arms to unfriendly states.[73] The English government was a little more sophisticated. Since English wool was greatly desired on the Continent, England could draw a large revenue from export duties on wool shipments. England could also punish enemies and reward friends by forbidding ex-

[73] The French began to impose such embargoes in the later 13th century; see *Ord.*, xi, 353; i, 324, 351, 422, 505. The English used embargoes as an economic weapon under Henry II. John definitely forbade the export of arms; see *Rot. lit. pat.*, pp. 42-43. For more details see my forthcoming article, "Notes on the Origin of Export Taxes."

port of wool to hostile or potentially hostile countries.[74] Finally, by manipulating export duties to favor manufactured cloth over raw wool, England stimulated the growth of a native woolen industry.[75] Another example of state intervention to increase production can be seen in Castille, where sheep raisers were given extensive rights of pasturage as they moved their flocks from summer to winter quarters.[76]

Nevertheless, all these attempts to regulate foreign trade produced very little in the form of administrative structures. Even England, which was more dependent on export duties than any other country, did not have an efficient or centralized customs service. At first, the customs were often pledged (in effect, farmed) to foreign or native bankers.[77] Even then the local customs collectors were usually merchants of the seaport towns, and such men remained collectors as the practice of pledging the customs as security for loans died out.[78] In the same way, the English gov-

[74] N.S.B. Gras, *The Early English Customs System* (Cambridge, Mass., 1918), p. 63; J. de Sturler, *Les relations politiques et les échanges commerciaux entre le duché de Brabant et l'Angleterre* (Paris, 1936), pp. 124-126; *Cambridge Economic History of Europe*, ed. M. M. Postan, E. E. Rich, E. Miller (Cambridge, Eng., 1963), III, pp. 313-316; G. Unwin, *Finance and Trade under Edward III* (Manchester, 1918).

[75] M. McKisack, *The Fourteenth Century* (Oxford, 1959), pp. 363-369; E. F. Jacob, *The Fifteenth Century* (Oxford, 1961), pp. 349-350; E. E. Power and M. M. Postan, *Studies in English Trade in the Fifteenth Century* (London, 1933); E. Power, *The Wool Trade in English Medieval History* (Oxford, 1941), p. 101-103.

[76] *Cambridge Economic History*, 2nd ed., ed. M. M. Postan (Cambridge, Eng., 1966), I, 132-133, 438-439.

[77] R. L. Baker, "The English Customs Service, 1307-1343," *Transactions of the American Philosophical Society*, n.s., LI, part 6 (1961), esp. pp. 10-14, 23-27.

[78] *The English Government at Work 1327-1336*, ed. W. A.

ernment in the end relied on an association of merchants (the Company of the Staple) to see that exports went only to authorized markets.[79] There was no single office in the central government responsible for the control of exports or the collection of export (and import) duties. France had a more centralized system, at least in theory, by the early fourteenth century. There were three (later reduced to one) general supervisors of exports; but they had an utterly inadequate staff, and the most active member of the group, Pierre de Chalon, was seldom in Paris.[80] The "master of ports and passages" continued to control exports and payment of export duties under the general supervision of the *Chambre des Comptes*. But his office was not very important; it produced little revenue and it had little effect on the economy of the country.[81]

The real puzzle is the slowness with which departments dealing with defense and foreign affairs developed. The chief business of most fourteenth-century governments was war. Wars were preceded by negotiations with probable adversaries and potential allies; they were interrupted by truces which also required careful negotiations; they were ended by peace treaties which not only involved long nego-

Morris and J. R. Strayer (Cambridge, Mass., 1947), II, pp. 27-31, and the chapter by Mabel H. Mills on the collectors; Baker, *English Customs Service*, pp. 43-49.

[79] E. Power, *Wool Trade*, pp. 86-103.

[80] J. R. Strayer, "Pierre de Chalon and the Origins of the French Customs Service," *Festschrift Percy Ernst Schramm* (Wiesbaden, 1964), I, 334-339.

[81] Rey, *Le domaine du roi*, pp. 54-55; *Cambridge Economic History*, III, 319; R. Doucet, *Institutions de la France au XVIe siècle* (Paris, 1948), II, 556.

tiations but also subsequent meetings to interpret the terms of the treaties. And yet generation after generation of war and negotiation failed to produce the institutions which one would have expected to emerge: War Offices and Foreign Offices.

It is easy enough to understand why specialized military departments had not appeared in the thirteenth century. From 1215 to the 1290's none of the larger states engaged in a major war. English raids on France were brushed off with no difficulty. Charles of Anjou conquered the kingdom of Sicily in a single battle. The French attack on Aragon in 1285 was limited to one brief, unsuccessful summer campaign. Even the bitter papal/Hohenstaufen conflict failed to develop into a large-scale war; most of the fighting was between rival Italian city-states and rival German princes. Permanent armies and War Offices were scarcely needed while hostilities remained at such low levels. The emerging states could concentrate on developing institutions for internal affairs.

On the other hand, the very peacefulness of the thirteenth century encouraged the growth of diplomacy. Louis IX of France settled his disputes with England and with Aragon by carefully prepared treaties, and these treaties required further negotiations to settle questions that remained obscure.[82] Both the popes and the Hohenstaufen carried on an active correspondence with the kings of England and France, and with lesser rulers in their efforts to secure active

[82] G. P. Cuttino, *English Diplomatic Administration 1259-1339* (Oxford, 1940), pp. 5-14; *Histoire générale de Langue doc*, VIII, *preuves*, col. 1519, x, col. 24.

support or benevolent neutrality.[83] The Italian towns and the German princes who were necessarily involved in the papal/Hohenstaufen struggle negotiated endlessly to gain maximum advantages for themselves at minimum risks. By the end of the century the kings of England and France were seeking the support of West German princes.[84] Even the Greeks and the Moslems were involved in this intensified diplomatic activity. Not to mention commercial treaties, Frederick II secured Jerusalem by a treaty;[85] Louis IX extricated himself from his Egyptian campaign by a treaty;[86] the abortive attack on Tunis in 1270 ended in a treaty that was very favorable to Charles I of Sicily;[87] and this same Charles was thwarted again and again in his efforts to attack the revived Byzantine Empire by the diplomacy of Michael Paleologus.[88] Perhaps the most striking example of the reliance of thirteenth-century Western European rulers on diplomacy was their reaction to the sudden appearance of the Mongols in the Middle East. Both the pope and Louis IX of France immediately sent embassies to

[83] F. Graese, *Die Publizistik in der letzen Epoche Kaiser Friedrichs II* (Heidelberg, 1909); H. Wieruszowski, *Vom Imperium zum Nationalen Königtum* (Munich and Berlin, 1933), pp. 58-65.

[84] F. Kern, *Die Anfänge der französischen Ausdehnungspolitik* (Tübingen, 1910), pp. 71-80; B. Lyon, *From Fief to Indenture* (Cambridge, Mass., 1957), pp. 161-180.

[85] T. C. Van Cleve, "The Crusade of Frederick II," in *A History of the Crusades,* ed. K. M. Setton (Philadelphia, 1962), II, 452-458.

[86] Joinville, *Histoire de St. Louis,* ed. Natalis de Wailly (Paris, 1874), pp. 186-200.

[87] *Chronique de Primat,* in *Recueil des historiens des Gaules et de la France,* XXIII, 79-80. See the comments of R. Sternfeld, *Ludwigs des Heiligen Kreuzzug nach Tunis* (Berlin, 1896), pp. 264-271.

[88] C. Chapman, *Michel Paléologue* (Paris, 1926).

the Great Khan, and throughout the rest of the century there were repeated efforts to arrange an alliance between Christians and Mongols against the Moslems. These efforts failed, but one eminent scholar thinks they might have succeeded if European rulers had been a little better informed about the East and a little more realistic in their policies.[89]

In short, by the end of the thirteenth century, there were lively diplomatic exchanges taking place in most parts of Western Europe. But diplomatic exchanges, numerous though they were, did not force the creation of separate departments of foreign affairs. The concept of "foreign affairs" could hardly exist in a Europe that admitted the fact that it was made up of a congeries of sovereign states but was not quite sure what states were sovereign. For example, a king of France might send letters on the same day to the count of Flanders, who was definitely his vassal but a very independent and unruly one, to the count of Luxemburg, who was a prince of the Empire but who held a money-fief (a regular, annual pension) of the king of France, and to the king of Sicily, who was certainly ruler of a sovereign state but was also a prince of the French royal house. In such a situation one could hardly distinguish between internal and external affairs. It seemed reasonable to allow the chancellor and his secretarial staff to handle all correspondence, whatever its nature, and to preserve records of all important acts without trying to set up a separate register for diplomatic correspondence.

By and large, if a department of government had

[89] R. Grousset, *Histoire des Croisades*, III (Paris, 1948), 518-530.

not been set up by the end of the thirteenth century, it was not apt to appear until the sixteenth or even the seventeenth century. This proved true of war and diplomacy. Administration of military affairs, preparation and preservation of diplomatic documents remained in the hands of the old financial and secretarial agencies. There was, of course, some specialization. There were treasurers for war, usually drawn from and returning to the ranks of a department of finance. Such men had general oversight of military expenditures, especially the payment of troops, and were aided by a reasonably large staff of clerks.[90] Because wars lasted so much longer than they had in earlier centuries, the post of treasurer for war became almost permanent. But the treasurer (or treasurers— there were often two or more) did not control a Ministry of War. They did not even control all military expenditures; many captains and companies made their own bargains with and drew their wages directly from king and Council.[91] The treasurer for war had very little to do with recruitment and had no responsibility whatever for operations. King and Council, with the advice of experienced commanders, determined such matters. In time of peace, the number of men concerned with military affairs dwindled rapidly. There was no standing army, except for a few understrength and poorly paid garrisons in key

[90] L. Mirot, "Dom Béry et les comptes des trésoriers des guerres," *Bib. de l'École des Chartes*, LXXXVI (1925), 245-379; H. Moranvillé, "Étude sur Jean le Mercier" (see note 72); Tout, *Chapters*, III, 73, 316, 338, 347-349, 396; IV, 225.

[91] F. Lot, *L'art militaire et les armées au Moyen Age* (Paris, 1946), I, 395-410; M. R. Powicke, "Lancastrian Captains," in Sandquist and Powicke, *Essays*, pp. 371-382.

castles. When the king ceased paying their wages, the companies of fighting men either dissolved or formed a small and dangerous private army under the captain who had recruited them. Such "free companies" were completely uncontrolled by any governmental agency, as their record of looting and destruction shows.

There was also some specialization in diplomacy. When a diplomatic controversy lasted for some time, it was natural that some official should be given continuing responsibility for keeping records of the negotiation. As Professor Cuttino has shown, in the long argument between England and France over the extent of the duchy of Aquitaine, there was usually an English king's clerk in charge of what we would call the "country desk": that is, a man who kept the file of documents dealing with the problem from its beginning.[92] At the operating end, it was not uncommon to keep certain experts on the negotiating team for several years at a time. But just as a treasurer for war did not make a War Office, so experts on Aquitaine, the papal curia, and so on did not make a Foreign Office. These experts were attached to permanent departments; most of them did not spend all their time on their diplomatic specialties, and they had very little influence on policy. They had rather precise instructions; they were to get what they could; if they failed they were not blamed. Foreign policy, like military policy, was controlled and determined by the king and Council.

Given the absence of earlier specialization, this attitude was understandable enough in the political atmosphere of the fourteenth century. The king may

[92] Cuttino, *English Diplomatic Administration*, pp. 19-48.

well have thought that war and diplomacy were matters too important to be entrusted to professional administrators. Certainly the prelates, princes of the blood, and great nobles, who were the dominant element in the Council in most states, felt that these were areas in which they had special responsibility and competence. They were indispensable as heads of diplomatic missions, governors of frontier areas, and commanders of armies. Unfortunately, as we have seen, they were precisely the men who were least willing to conform to administrative routine. They wanted to deal directly with the king; they wanted to be exempted from any regular procedures of accounting and reporting. Aristocratic privilege remained an enemy of administrative efficiency for many centuries, and nowhere was this more true than in the fields of military operations and diplomatic negotiations. The magnates disliked the institutionalization and professionalization of these functions of government, and their resistance explains in part the slow development of specialized and effective departments for military and foreign affairs.

As suggested above, rulers shared these prejudices to some extent. They wanted ambassadors to report directly to them and not to a secretary; they wanted to plan and direct their wars in person. They took it for granted that only a bishop or a great noble could represent them properly on an embassy, just as they took it for granted that princes and nobles were the only proper people to command military forces. They were probably also concerned about the expense of permanent military or diplomatic establishments. The aristocrat was always available for emergencies and did not have to be paid in times of peace or when there was a lull in negotiations. He often supplied some of his staff at his own expense or paid his followers out of his own pocket, while waiting for wages which were always in arrears. It is true that the services of the aristocracy cost a great deal more in practice than they did in theory; everyone who had the ear of the king wanted gifts, pensions, and grants of land. But they would have demanded these gratifications in any case, and it was as well to get some work in return for them. If the financial departments of governments had been able to supply regular and adequate revenues, it probably would have been cheaper to have kept a skeleton military establishment and a small diplomatic corps in being year in and year out. But taxes came in slowly and in insufficient amounts; debts rose steadily, and every state suffered periods of financial exhaustion in which it had to cut all expenses sharply. It is doubtful if any medieval state could have supported even a small permanent army. A corps of diplomats in more or less permanent residence at the principal courts of Western Europe would have been relatively inexpensive, but, as we have seen, such a professional group would have lacked the authority to conduct important negotiations. Even the Venetians, who led in the development of new diplomatic techniques, were relatively slow in creating a group of resident ambassadors.[93] Meanwhile, contacts among European states remained intermittent; ambassadors were sent out on specific missions and returned

[93] D. E. Queller, *The Office of Ambassador in the Middle Ages* (Princeton, 1967), pp. 78-84; Garrett Mattingly, "The First Resident Embassies," *Speculum*, xii (1937), 425-433.

home when their work was finished, or interrupted. There was no permanent Foreign Office.

To sum up, while there were probably more professional bureaucrats in European states in 1450 than in 1300 there were not many new bureaus, or at least, not many new types of bureaus. The bureaucrats were more expert, more sophisticated in their own routines, but they were not better informed or more influential in making policy decisions than their thirteenth-century predecessors. The actual policymakers—the lords of the Council—were ignorant, selfish, and impulsive. There was a wide gap between the professional administrators and the policymakers.

iii

𝕴𝖙 𝖒𝖆𝖞 𝖘𝖊𝖊𝖒 that the European states had accomplished very little during the period 1300-1450; that indeed, they were less effective political instruments in 1450 than they had been in 1300. This appearance, however, is deceptive. In the first place they had survived, which was no small feat considering the troubles of the later Middle Ages. Second, they had preserved their basic administrative structures, even if they had not expanded and improved those structures as much as might have been desirable. Third, repeated crises had pointed out weaknesses in organization and procedure so clearly that few politically conscious men could be unaware of them. In short, European states had gained time and experience, both of them valuable commodities for a body politic.

The sudden change in the political atmosphere in the late fifteenth century is therefore not as inexplicable as it sometimes appears to be. All that was needed was an easing of earlier strains, a breathing space in which the lessons learned during the last century could be applied. On the purely material side, the economic and political situation improved after 1450. There were still years of depression and periods of violence; but over the long run the European economy was expanding again, and the frequency of warfare was decreasing. Most of the transalpine countries were reasonably prosperous by the last quarter of the fifteenth century. Civil wars petered out with

89

the defeat of Charles of Burgundy in France, the accession of Ferdinand and Isabella in Spain, and the victory of the Tudors in England. After the end of the Hundred Years' War in 1453, international conflicts became, for a while, less intense. England avoided any serious war for over a century; France and Spain squabbled over Italy but did not engage in full-scale hostilities until well after 1500. Thus the "New Monarchs" had time, money, and energy to devote to the work of strengthening their governments.

They also had the support of a large majority of their subjects. It is not surprising that the poorer classes wanted security and good government; these were old desires, constantly expressed and constantly disappointed. Their frustration had led to hopeless rebellions in the fourteenth and fifteenth centuries; their partial satisfaction gave a little more stability to sixteenth-century governments. But peasant-artisan uprisings had not been nearly as dangerous as the disaffection of the propertied classes, and the really crucial change was in the attitudes of the baronage, the country gentlemen, and the town oligarchies. These groups remained restless, jealous of their privileges, and somewhat suspicious of the central government. Some of them were still ready to risk open rebellion rather than to accept official acts of which they disapproved. But the majority of the privileged classes was now ready to cooperate with the government and to accept royal leadership with an enthusiasm that had been rare for the last century. The growth of court ceremonial, of the majesty that surrounds a king, was but an outward sign of an increase in respect for the power and authority of the ruler. Adulation of the monarch came long before theories of divine right, just as recognition of the king's unique executive power came several generations before Bodin formulated his doctrine of sovereignty. In fact, both divine right and sovereignty were attempts to find theological or legal terms to explain and justify a change that had already taken place in the position of the head of the state. Once these doctrines had been formulated, they reinforced already existing attitudes towards monarchy, but the attitudes existed before the doctrines.

It is difficult to decide what factors changed the behavior of the possessing classes. Some of them, especially the lesser landholders, had suffered as much from internal violence as had the poor, and like the poor, wanted peace and security. Some of them realized that they could profit most fully from the economic revival that was beginning by supporting stable governments. Some of them may have been impressed by the failure of most late fifteenth-century rebellions. Whatever the reason, the possessing classes, on balance, assisted rather than resisted their governments during the crucial years at the end of the fifteenth and the beginning of the sixteenth century. Granted this change in attitudes, very small reforms at the center could produce disproportionately large effects in the state as a whole.

This is the reason why historians can find so little that is new in the so-called "New Monarchies." There was no need to create new institutions if the old institutions could be made to work better. There was no need to use force when most of the subjects were ready to obey of their own free will. The creation of standing armies, emphasized by some historians, was more important for external than internal affairs.[94] England had no standing army; the French standing army was small and stationed mainly on the frontiers; the Spanish standing army was usually occupied in Italy, the Empire, or the Netherlands. Neither administrative gimmicks nor military power explain the success of the sixteenth-century state. Intelligent use of existing resources and increased cooperation between rulers and subjects were the essential ingredients of the "New Monarchies."

We have seen that a basic weakness of the late medieval state was the gap between policymakers and professional officials. Policymakers were ill-informed, self-seeking, and erratic in their decisions. Bureaucrats were unimaginative, caught up in rigid routines, uninformed on some essential points, and not always in a position to control local leaders. The kings of the late fifteenth century quite sensibly decided that it was easier to reform the policymakers than the bureaucrats. They needed only a dozen or so policymakers, while they had to have thousands of bureaucrats; there were only a few hundred policy decisions to make each year as opposed to tens of thousands of routine judicial, financial, and administrative rulings.

Moreover, the policymaking process was centered in the Council, and the amorphous nature of the Council made it easy to reform. The ruler was entirely free to determine its membership and its duties. All that was needed was to find a few able men, put them to work, and let them stay at work long enough

[94] See J. Russell Major's remarks on the French army in *Representative Institutions in Renaissance France* (Madison, 1960), pp. 9-10.

to acquire the necessary knowledge and skills. The Council could still look very much as it always had, especially on formal occasions. It might officially include the princes of the blood, the leading prelates and nobles, and the great officers of state. But within the formal Council was a working Council (or Councils—duties were sometimes divided among two or more groups) which became more and more professionalized. It was drawn largely from the lower levels of the privileged classes, from the lesser aristocracy, and from government clerks. The higher nobility were excluded because to be a member of the working Council was a fulltime and often long-term job. A really expert councillor would be retained by successive sovereigns with very different points of view. In France Florimond Robertet served Charles VIII, Louis XII, and Francis I;[95] in England William Paget began his career under Henry VIII, held influential posts under Edward VI and Mary, and was consulted on important occasions by Elizabeth.[96] Perhaps an even more difficult task was to retain the confidence of the same ruler over many years, but the experience of the Cecils under Queen Elizabeth showed that it could be done. And even the professional councillors who fell from favor after relatively short periods of service usually had time to leave their mark on policy.

The members of the Council who remained amateurs, who did not work full-time, gradually lost most of their influence. A few who had expert knowledge

[95] G. Robertet, *Les Robertets au XVIᵉ siècle* (Paris, 1888).
[96] Paget was a Secretary of State in 1543, Comptroller of the Household 1547, Keeper of the Privy Seal 1555, a former clerk of the Council, and an influential member of the Council under Edward and Mary.

on a particular problem might be consulted from time to time, but they were advisers, not policymakers. Policy was made by the ruler and by a small number of professional councillors—seldom more than ten or twelve, often as few as three or four.

The professionalization of the inner Council had two important results. The first is obvious; the policymakers had more opportunities to become well-informed and more reason to weigh their judgments carefully. The second was a natural result of the heavy responsibilities they carried; they needed a supporting staff of clerks, informants, and agents. Thus a new bureaucracy began to crystallize around the professional members of the Council, a bureaucracy that was more amenable to the wishes of the ruler and more flexible in its procedures than the old, corporate bureaucracy inherited from the Middle Ages.

The best example of these changes can be found in the development of the office of the Secretary of State.[97] The Secretaries (there were usually two or more of them) were the most professional, and often

[97] For the Secretaries in England, see J. Otway-Ruthven, *The King's Secretary and the Signet Office in the Fifteenth Century* (Cambridge, Eng., 1939); F.M.G. Evans, *The Principal Secretary of State 1558-1680* (Manchester, 1923); and the remarkable studies of Conyers Read, *Mr. Secretary Cecil and Queen Elizabeth* (New York, 1955), *Mr. Secretary Walsingham*, 3 vols. (Cambridge, Mass., 1925). An interesting contemporary description of the duties of the Secretary may be found in the last-named work, I, 423-443. For France the old work of Fauvelet du Toc, *Histoire des Secrétaires d'Estat* (Paris, 1668), is still useful. See also H. de Luçay, *Des origines du pouvoir ministériel en France: Les Secrétaires d'Etat depuis leur institution jusqu'à la mort de Louis XV* (Paris, 1881); and N. M. Sutherland, *The French Secretaries of State in the Age of Catherine de Medici* (London, 1962).

the most powerful members of the inner Council. Originally private secretaries of the ruler, they started with more information about the affairs of state than any other councillors. Since they prepared the letters that expressed the king's will, they were often called on to translate policy decisions into action. They retained their close personal relationship with the sovereign long after they became public officers, which meant that they knew better than anyone else the wishes of the man who made the final decisions. The prestige and authority of the Secretaries grew steadily during the later part of the fifteenth century, and ambitious and capable men clustered around them, seeking office and influence. It was out of such groups that the new departments of government eventually developed.

The new departments, however, were a long way off in the sixteenth century. Meanwhile the Secretaries had far too much to do and far too little staff assistance. Their primary duty was to preserve the security of the state against internal and external enemies. They had very little to work with in the way of armed force. As we have seen, England had no standing army, and the armies of other states were small and scattered. No country had an adequate police force, and local militias, or levies of country gentlemen were effective only against groups as ill-trained and unorganized as they were. Internal security was preserved not by the use of force, but by the acquisi-

---

For individual careers, see J. Nouaillic, *Villeroy, Secrétaire d'Etat et ministre de Charles IX, Henri III et Henri IV* (Paris, 1888), and the book on the Robertets cited in note 95.

tion of timely knowledge and the establishment of a network of personal relationships between the Secretaries (and other working members of the Council) and influential local men. Information, suggestions, propaganda, and directives passed from the center down to local notables; information, requests, and warnings went up the line to the Council. The system was far from perfect; but in the sixteenth century a great deal more was known about local conditions, and a great deal more reliance could be placed on local authorities than in the fifteenth.

Outside threats to security were handled in somewhat the same way. Again the emphasis was on acquiring information.[98] Permanent embassies were established; secret agents and spies were hired; knowledgeable merchants and travellers were questioned. As far as possible, personal relationships were established with influential or well-informed men in foreign countries. The results were probably less good in foreign than in domestic affairs; a great deal of nonsense was reported by men who should have known better, and there were few governments that were not shockingly deceived by foreign rulers from time to time. Nevertheless, there was improvement throughout the century, both in the quality of information and in the decisions derived from it.

The effort to obtain exact and early information was one of the signs of the emergence of a new type of policymaker. But we should not forget that the

[98] See the tract on the duties of a Secretary cited in note 97; E. H. Harbison, *Rival Ambassadors at the Court of Queen Mary* (Princeton, 1940); Garrett Mattingly, *Renaissance Diplomacy* (New York, 1955).

efforts were not well-coordinated and that they were not adequately supported by governments. Even the Secretaries had remarkably small staffs and limited funds, and other members of the Council were given even less help. Because power went to the well-informed, ambitious men used their own assets, social and financial, to acquire information. Because power, prestige, and perhaps wealth could come from close contacts with the Council, young men were willing to act as assistants to Council members for little or no pay. But while governments saved money by relying on the ambition and resources of private persons, they slowed down the professionalization of key areas of administration, such as diplomacy and military affairs. The small professional element that was beginning to appear in the Council had to depend to a large degree on the support of amateurs and part-time workers. This mixture of amateur and professional is one reason why it took so long for well-organized departments of government to emerge from the inner Council. But it is hard to see how the mixture could have been avoided, as long as governments could not, or believed that they could not, pay for large professional staffs.

Another problem was to coordinate the work of the still amorphous new bureaucracy with that of the well-established old bureaucracy. There was bound to be some friction, of course. No government has ever been able to eliminate interdepartmental rivalries, and the rivalries are apt to be especially great when a new department is trying to find a place for itself in a rigid administrative structure. The most obvious example of this kind of rivalry in the sixteenth and

seventeenth centuries was in the courts of law. All
European rulers of any consequence had reserved
certain rights of justice for themselves, even when
they allowed the vast majority of cases to be settled
by their professional judges. By the end of the fifteenth century and even more in the sixteenth century, rulers were exploiting these reserved rights more
vigorously than they had earlier. The Council, a committee of the Council, or an individual member of the
Council, acting in the ruler's name, could try cases
that touched the security of the state, or cases in
which strict application of the law threatened to work
injustice. England perhaps saw this process most completely institutionalized in the creation of Conciliar
courts such as the Court of Star Chamber or the Court
of Requests, and this may be one reason why protests
against prerogative courts were especially vehement
in England.[99] But many French officials were unhappy about the special commissions or Chambers
set up by the king to try important cases, and there
were a considerable number of *Ordonnances* that
tried to regulate or limit the king's reserved rights of
justice.[100]

One could find other examples of friction among
officials of the central government, for example, in
problems of finance; but their importance should not
be exaggerated. As we have seen, the working Council was small and understaffed; it could not have taken
over all the work of the old bureaucracy, even if it
had wanted to do so. Conversely the old bureaucracy

[99] W. S. Holdsworth, *History of English Law* (Boston, 1922),
I, 414-415, 459-465, 508-514.
[100] J. Declareuil, *Histoire Générale du Droit Français* (Paris,
1925), pp. 664-666.

was fully occupied with the routine business of government; it not very eager to experiment with the new procedures or to assume the heavy responsibilities of the Council. Even in the administration of justice, the point of greatest friction, there was a considerable amount of cooperation between the ordinary courts and the Conciliar courts. Judges of the older courts found some advantages in letting other men decide difficult or politically dangerous cases.

A greater problem for the new bureaucracy was that of dealing with local or regional authorities. Many of these men were local notables, just professional enough to take refuge behind the fixed rules and procedures of their offices but just amateur enough to have little desire for promotion, especially for promotion that would require them to leave home. Such men were not apt to enforce directives of the central government with undue rigor. The members of most town governments and most rural magistrates fell in this category of local notables; in England almost all local officials were of this type. Elsewhere, particularly in France, there were local judges and administrators who were thoroughly professional, in the sense of having had some training for their jobs and some desire to advance in the service of the king. But even these men were often imbued with local prejudices and defended local or regional privileges as zealously as the town oligarchs and rural squires of England.[101] All policy decisions of the Council had to be

[101] R. Mousnier, *Les XVIe et XVIIe siècles* (Paris, 1954), p. 164: "Il s'agissait de savoir qui allait administrer le royaume: des fonctionnaires royaux nommés et revoqués à volonté . . . ou des corps d'officiers propriétaires de leur charges, done peu maniables et pratiquement irrévocables, plus soucieux des

filtered through this layer of local leaders and officials, and in the process essential ingredients were often eliminated. Well into the seventeenth century the best-organized states were in a sense only federations of counties or provinces, and each unit of the federation adapted orders from the center to fit its own needs.

There was no quick way to solve this problem. There were not enough professional administrators to govern the whole country directly from the center; there was not enough money to pay them if they had existed; there was not enough sense of unity to make their presence tolerable when they were introduced. The French intendants of the seventeenth century met strong resistance and were never as powerful as they pretended to be. One of the most hated memories of the Cromwellian period in England was the rule of the Major-Generals. Early modern Europe was not yet ready for real centralization. One of the latest of the new departments to develop was an effective Ministry of the Interior.

Given the difficulties, most European governments coped with the problem of regional and local particularism fairly intelligently. As was said earlier, members of the central government tried to keep in touch with provincial leaders by correspondence, and to keep an eye on them through spies and informants. It might not be possible to coerce local notables, but it was often possible to gain their support by grants

intérêts qu'ils représentent que de l'utilité publique . . . alliés de nobles d'épée, devenus des puissances provinciales ou locales . . . représentant plus les provinces et les intérêts particuliers en face du roi que le roi devant les intérêts particuliers et les provinces. . . ."

of honors or by favors to their families and friends. A good deal of local non-conformity could simply be overlooked, as long as it was not too blatant. And in the last resort, military force could be used against a group or a region that had overstepped the bounds of permissiveness. It was not possible to punish all the disobedient or recalcitrant, but examples could be made of notorious offenders.

Tenuous and indirect though it was, control of the provinces by the central governments of the western kingdoms was reasonably effective in the sixteenth and seventeenth centuries. All regional rebellions were sooner or later suppressed. Orders of the courts were enforced, even if slowly, and individual security increased. Taxes were collected regularly. They did not yield as much as governments would have liked nor were they designed so as to get at the real wealth of subjects. But while early modern states, like their medieval predecessors, were always short of money, they could do more before they approached the edge of bankruptcy. They spent more for palaces and other evidences of royal splendor, more for administrative expenses, more for war and diplomacy. And most of the money they spent was provided, however grudgingly, by men working for the government at the local level.

Finally, the new bureaucracy had a certain amount of difficulty in dealing with its creator, the king or the prince. Rulers were jealous of their power; they did not want to create departments that would become autonomous, self-perpetuating, and difficult to control. Especially they did not want such departments in areas traditionally reserved for the personal decisions of the ruler, such as war, diplomacy, and internal security. The real mark of sovereignty was now possession of executive power. The old idea that sovereignty was primarily the right to give final decisions in justice was far from dead—witness the famous preamble to Henry VIII's Act in Restraint of Appeals.[102] The new idea that sovereignty could be found in the right to make law certainly affected the conduct of governments. Early modern states legislated more, and their legislation touched a wider range of human activities (for example religion) than that of medieval states. But the political crises of the sixteenth and seventeenth centuries were not caused by disputes over legislative power; they were caused by disputes over the possession and extent of executive power. Most rulers asserted that they alone had the right to make whatever decisions were necessary to preserve or strengthen the state. They resented any attempts to limit or control this power. It was an intensely personal possession; others could advise but only the ruler could decide.

Thus a sixteenth- or seventeenth-century king faced an annoying dilemma. He needed expert councillors, men with knowledge and experience who could solve all problems and foresee all dangers. But the more nearly a councillor approached this ideal the more likely he was to start making his own decisions rather than defer to the king. Again, intelligent and consistent policies could not be devised or executed if the working members of the Council were

[102] *Statutes of the Realm*, III, 427ff; the king, who wears the "imperial crown" of England has "plenary, whole and entire power . . . to render and yield justice and final determination to all manner of folk residents or subjects within his realm. . . ."

102

supported only by an inadequate, partly amateur staff. But to give adequate staff support to the men who ran foreign and military affairs meant to create powerful bureaucratic groups that might deprive the monarch of some of his powers of decision—as the judges had long ago deprived him of most of his power to make legal decisions. One can understand why rulers were a little suspicious of their expert advisers even though they recognized the need for expertise.

A solution that allowed the monarch to use experienced, more or less professional councillors freely without delegating too much power to any one of them was to adopt the principle of collegialty. Thus there might be several Secretaries of State, or a Council Committee on foreign affairs, or boards to regulate trade and administer colonies. In both France and England, for example, direction of foreign affairs was for a time divided among two, three, or four Secretaries. Each Secretary was responsible for a certain geographical area. In seventeenth-century England one Secretary was in charge of relations with northern countries, the other of relations with southern countries, including the American colonies.[103] In France in the sixteenth century there were four Secretaries; each was responsible for internal security for a section of France and for relations with foreign countries bordering on, or closest to, his section.[104] Obviously under such a system there could be no Foreign Secretary and no Foreign Office to interfere with the monarch's direct control of foreign affairs.

[103] Evans, *Principal Secretary of State*, pp. 131-136, 261-267, 323-328.
[104] Declareuil, *Hist. Gen. du Droit Français*, p. 471.

Faced with all these obstacles, it is not surprising that it took the new bureaucracy two or three centuries to develop solidly organized departments with clearly defined areas of responsibility. It is a little startling to observe that the process went no faster in the early modern period than it had in the Middle Ages. The first semi-professional judges appear in England in the 1130's; by 1250, when Bracton was writing his famous treatise on English law, central law courts manned by professionally trained judges were fully developed. The French began a little later, but it took them less than a century and a half to build the *Parlement* of Paris out of the undifferentiated, largely amateur *curia regis*. The new departments (foreign affairs, war, etc.) developed more rapidly in France than in other kingdoms, but even in France nearly a century and a half passed between the appearance of the first powerful Secretaries and the establishment of a Foreign Office on a permanent basis. England was even slower, and did not unite the conduct of all foreign affairs in the hands of a single Secretary until 1782. Similar delays can be found in the organization of a single office for military affairs and even greater delays in creating ministries for home affairs. Taking Europe as a whole, the full array of new departments of government can scarcely be said to have appeared before the beginning of the nineteenth century.

This slow growth of new departments caused a great deal of confusion and inefficiency. Authority was divided, and even with the best will in the world the divided authorities found it difficult to cooperate.

When there was ill will, as there often was, petty quarrels caused interminable delays, and made it almost impossible to execute the policies of the ruler. If European states began to dominate the world in the early modern period, it certainly was not because they had perfected their administrative organization. Rather one would have to say that the administrative systems of European states between the end of the Middle Ages and the French Revolution were just barely adequate, that every new internal or external crisis strained them severely.

Barely adequate, however, is quite different from failure. By remaining politically solvent, the European states gradually increased their political capital. And it should be remembered that the structure of European states, imperfect though it was, was considerably stronger than that of most of the overseas political communities with which Europeans had to deal. There was nothing in the Americas, nothing in India or the East Indies, and nothing in most of Africa that had the cohesion and endurance of a European state. And if the broad belt of Asian empires, stretching from Turkey through Persia to China and Japan could rival European states in organization and power up to the end of the eighteenth century, still the European states were improving their apparatus of government while the structures of the Asian empires were beginning to weaken.

The European states thus ran no danger from the slow development of essential institutions. At times they even profited from the looseness of their administrative system. For example, the division of power between the old bureaucrats and the new, professionalized breed of policymakers was not necessarily disadvantageous. Routine tasks were performed in a routine way by men who wanted to do nothing more than follow routine, while the policymakers could concentrate on important and unusual problems. If leaders of the propertied classes were not always entirely responsive to orders of the central government, at the same time they saved the government trouble and expense by assuming certain political burdens. The founding of colonies was a conspicuous example of well-to-do men performing a function that seemed desirable to, but beyond the resources of, early modern states. We should also remember that in most countries local notables were still responsible for enforcing many of the regulations affecting the economy, for arresting criminals, and for providing social services. The possessing classes did not always perform these functions very efficiently or very honestly, but they did perform them in an age when the state could not have performed them at all. And perhaps more significant than the actual performance of the work was the involvement of larger numbers of men in the political process. Just as the second stage of feudalism had given the lesser vassals a chance to participate in the work of government as judges and administrators, so the second stage of bureaucracy gave the rural and urban middle class the same sort of opportunity. The reasons were similar in both cases: the old ruling class could not furnish enough men to do all the work that had to be done, and so new men had to be drawn in.

The structure of the state varied widely from country to country in sixteenth- and seventeenth-century

Europe. Some states (notably seventeenth-century France) were fairly well-organized, some (notably seventeenth-century Russia) were barely able to survive. Careful planning and deliberate imitation reduced but did not eliminate these differences in the period after 1700. By the nineteenth century, administrative structures looked very much alike in most European (and European-derived) states, though surface resemblances hid profound differences in morale and efficiency. But by the nineteenth century even the weaker European states were better organized, better able to use their human and material resources, than the strong states of earlier periods.

Organization alone, however, could not have produced the modern state. As we have seen, the relatively badly organized states of the early sixteenth century were able to break out of a pattern of instability and civil war because a shift in attitudes produced greater loyalty to the ruler and to the state. The better organized states of the seventeenth century still had to deal with the problems of disobedience and civil war, and, like their predecessors, profited from the changing attitudes of subjects. Personal loyalty to the ruler reached its peak in the doctrine of divine right. If only one man, clearly designated by God, had the right to rule a particular country at a given moment, then all right-thinking people ought to obey him without question. In earlier periods men could accept the idea that monarchy was the best form of government without believing that all commands of a particular monarch had to be obeyed, or that any one monarch was irreplaceable. Acceptance of the theory of divine right monarchy made resistance il-

107

legitimate and so strengthened the state. For those who were sceptical about the divine right of monarchs there was the theory that the state was absolutely necessary for human welfare, and that that concentration of power which we call sovereignty was essential for the existence of the state. Men could not live a decent life—in fact, according to Hobbes they could not live at all—unless they lived in and obeyed the commands of a sovereign state. To weaken or to destroy the state was to threaten the future of the human race. Therefore a state was entitled to take any steps to ensure its own survival, even if those steps seemed unjust or cruel.

It was this second viewpoint that was most widely accepted. Opponents of existing regimes could get around or, if necessary, override the argument of divine right. It was not very clear, even to a true believer, who was the rightful king of Spain in 1700; one could support either candidate with a clear conscience. It did not seem to worry a majority of Englishmen in 1700 that their king could not claim to rule by divine right; they obeyed him rather better than they had the previous king, who *had* ruled by divine right. But even in England, where monarchy had been weakened and legal restraints had been imposed on arbitrary acts of government, no politically important group doubted that the state had to be preserved and strengthened. Thus in time of war the landholding class accepted a fairly steep tax on its property, even though it was the most influential political group in the country. Loyalty to the state made up for many weaknesses in administrative organization.

Loyalty to the state was soon to be tested by the emergence of the idea of nationalism. Where nation and state coincided fairly closely, there were no particular problems. But where a national group had been split into many states, as in Germany, or where a state embraced many national groups, as in the Habsburg domains, there was bound to be a conflict between the old and the new loyalties.[105] The settlement of this conflict lies beyond the scope of the present essay; in fact, it is clear that the conflict is not going to reach a final solution in this century. For our purposes the question is whether nationalism was beginning to reinforce—or to challenge—loyalty to the European states that existed in the seventeenth century.

Evidence on this point is hard to find. Nationalism is a vague term: when does it begin to be something more than mere xenophobia, how does it differ from the old local and regional loyalties, what are its connections with religious, cultural and linguistic differences? About all that we can say is that in the seventeenth century there are some signs of what might be called nationalism in the long-established kingdoms of England, France, and Spain, and that such nationalism as existed tended to strengthen those states. Elsewhere, nationalism was not yet strong enough to disrupt existing states or to prevent consolidation of imperfectly united states. Thus the Scots, who certainly were strongly attached to their own institutions and way of life, accepted an organic union with England in 1707, and Magyar and Czech resentment of Aus-

[105] See Karl Deutsch and William J. Foltz, eds., *Nation-Building* (New York, 1963), especially the first three articles by Deutsch, Strayer, and Friedrich.

trian domination did not prevent the Habsburg lands from drawing closer together. There was more trouble in Spain, where the Catalans were constantly threatening rebellion, and where Portugal regained her independence in 1640 after a brief period of subjection to the Spanish king. But the union of the Iberian peninsula under one ruler was a very recent event. Portugal and Catalonia had had centuries in which to develop their own traditions, and it is perhaps more remarkable that most of the country remained under one ruler than that Portugal seceded. Moreover, some of the resistance to the authorities in Madrid might better be described as regionalism rather than nationalism, an attempt to preserve local privileges rather than an attempt to create a separate nation-state.

By 1700 the Western European state had developed its own characteristic political patterns, patterns that determine the structure of most states today. The techniques for building organized and specialized departments of government were well understood, even if many departments were still in an embryonic stage. A competent bureaucracy existed, and a workable relationship between bureaucrats and policymakers had been established. External affairs were at last being treated with some of the same skill that had long characterized the treatment of internal affairs. Sheer pressure of business and the need for securing the cooperation of the propertied classes had steadily increased the size of the group involved in the political process. The European state of the seventeenth century was far from being a democracy, but it was also far from being a despotism ruled by a monarch and a few cronies. Policy had to be explained and justified to the thousands of members of the ruling classes; due process of law had to be followed in all but exceptional cases. Finally, and perhaps most importantly, the state had become a necessity of life. It had gained the primary loyalty of its subjects. The intensity of loyalty varied, but even those who gave only passive obedience could not conceive of a world without a state. Western Europe was psychologically prepared for a strengthening of the organization and an increase in the functions of the state. Policies might be attacked; governments might be overthrown; but political convulsions could no longer destroy the concept of the state.

INDEX

113

Louis IX, 81, 82
loyalty to state, 9, 10, 45-46, 54-56, 107-109

Marmousets, 76
ministerials, 28
Mongols, 82-83

nationalism, 10, 109-110
"New Monarchies," 90, 92
nobles, 74-76, 86-87, 93
nomads, 6
Normandy, 17, 20, 32, 50
Northmen, 15, 16

Paget, William, 93
Parlement, 72-73, 104
Parliament, 45, 48
peace, 16, 30
Peace Movement, 19-20
Philip Augustus, 50-51
Pierre de Chalon, 80
policymakers, 74-76, 88, 92, 94
pope, 8, 21, 46-47, 53, 54-56, 81, 82
possession, 30, 40
prévôts, 28, 29
provinces, 49-51
provinces, absence of in England, 36-37, 47

representative assemblies, 64-68
revenue, 28-29, 69-71
Richard I, 42-43
Robertet, Florimond, 93
Rome, 11, 13

Samo, 13
Scotland, 59, 109
scutage, 44
Secretaries of State, 94-97, 103
sheriffs, 8, 28, 29, 37, 41, 52
Sicily, 35, 81
sovereignty, 9, 16, 42-44, 53, 58, 61, 83, 91, 102, 108
Spain, 35, 60, 110
Stapledon, Bishop, 72

taxation, 43-44, 46-47, 54-55, 67-68, 70-71, 101
tax-farmers, 73
Treasurer for war, 86
Treasury, 33

Wales, 51, 59
Walton Ordinances, 76
War Office, 84
wars, 58-60, 81, 90
witnesses, 41
writs, 41-42

114